Power Maths

Year 5 Textb

Series Editor: Tony Staneff

M000316379

Sparks

Sparks is helpful and supportive.

He will remind you of things that may help you.

flexible

Flo

curious

Ash

brave

Astrid

determined

Dexter

Pearson

Contents

Your teacher will tell you which page you need.

Get ready …
set … let's learn
maths together!

How to use this book

These pages make sure we're ready for the unit ahead. Find out what we'll be learning and brush up on your skills!

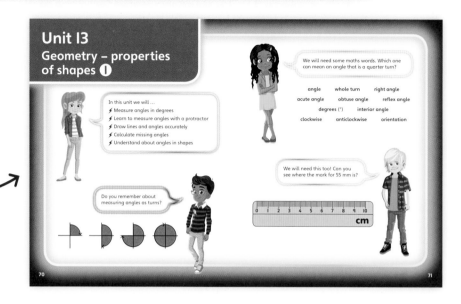

Discover

Lessons start with **Discover**.

Here, we explore new maths problems.

Can you work out how to find the answer?

Don't be afraid to make mistakes. Learn from them and try again!

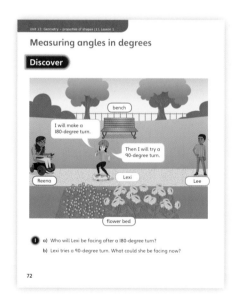

Share

Next, we share our ideas with the class.

Did we all solve the problems the same way? What ideas can you try?

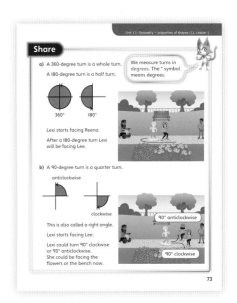

Think together

Then we have a go at some more problems together. Use what you have just learnt to help you.

We'll try a challenge too!

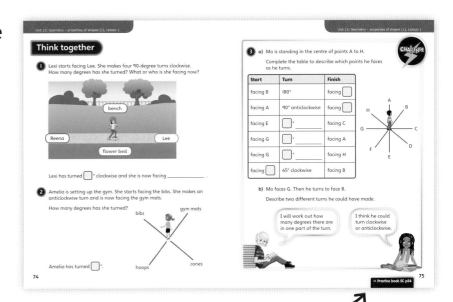

This tells you which page to go to in your **Practice Book**.

At the end of each unit there's an **End of unit check**. This is our chance to show how much we have learnt.

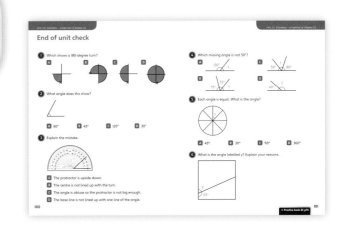

Unit 12
Decimals

In this unit we will ...

⚡ Add and subtract decimals with the same number of digits after the decimal point

⚡ Add and subtract decimals with a different number of digits after the decimal point

⚡ Add whole numbers to decimals

⚡ Subtract decimals from whole numbers

⚡ Solve problems involving addition and subtraction of decimals including money problems

⚡ Multiply and divide decimals and whole numbers by 10, 100 and 1,000

We will need to use column methods. How can we add these two numbers?

H	T	O
100	10 10	1 1 1 1 1 1 1
	10 10 10 10 10 10 10	1 1 1 1 1

```
  H T O
    1 2 6
  +   7 5
  -------
```

We will need some maths words.
Do you know what they all mean?

add   subtract   decimal   tenths

hundredths   thousandths   multiply

divide   decimal point   whole

column   exchange   place value

decimal place   digit

We also need to be able to subtract numbers.

Can you remember a way of making 500 − 367 easier?

Why are these two calculations the same?

```
  H  T  O
  5  0  0
− 3  6  7
_____
```

```
  H  T  O
  4  9  9
− 3  6  6
_____
```

Adding and subtracting decimals ❶

Discover

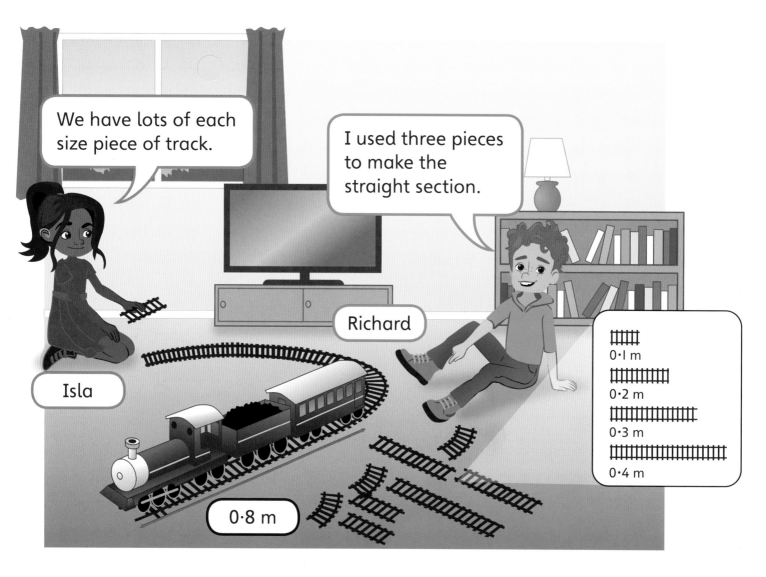

We have lots of each size piece of track.

I used three pieces to make the straight section.

Richard

Isla

0·1 m
0·2 m
0·3 m
0·4 m

0·8 m

❶ **a)** Which pieces of track could Richard have used to make the straight section?

b) Isla uses different pieces of track.

What other ways could Isla have made a track of 0·8 m?

Share

a) There are track pieces 0·1 m, 0·2 m, 0·3 m and 0·4 m long.

We need to find three pieces that add up to 0·8 m.

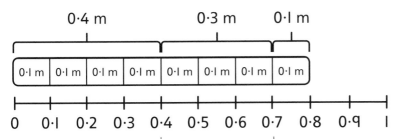

> I used a bar model to work out the possible pieces.

0·4 m + 0·3 m + 0·1 = 0·8 m

Richard could have used 0·4 m, 0·3 m and 0·1 m track pieces to make the straight section.

b) There are several possible answers.

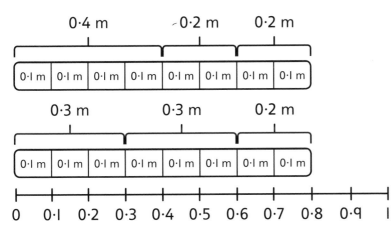

0·4 + 0·2 + 0·2 = 0·8

Isla could have used one 0·4 m and two 0·2 m pieces.

Or she could have used two 0·3 m and one 0·2 m pieces to make a track of 0·8 m.

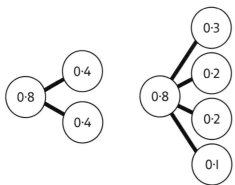

> I have found other answers which add to 8 tenths.

Think together

1 **a)** These pieces of track (A and B) are put together.

How long is the track in total?

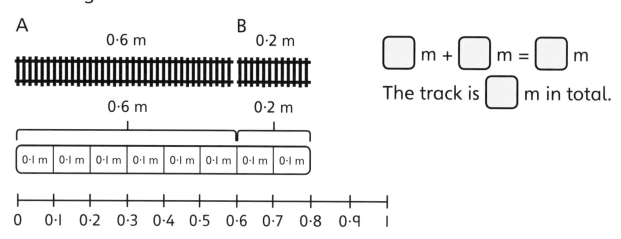

$\boxed{}$ m + $\boxed{}$ m = $\boxed{}$ m

The track is $\boxed{}$ m in total.

b) How much longer is track piece A than B?

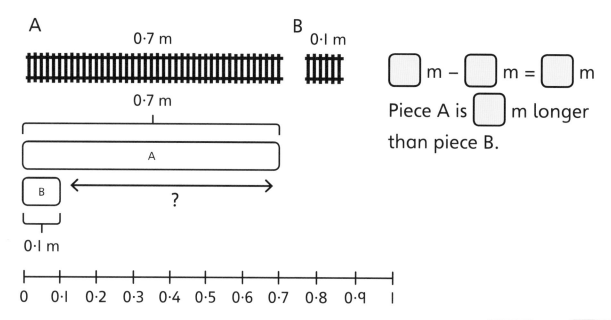

$\boxed{}$ m − $\boxed{}$ m = $\boxed{}$ m

Piece A is $\boxed{}$ m longer than piece B.

2 **a)** Which two numbers add up to 0·9?

b) Which cards have a difference of 0·1?

c) Which two cards add up to 0·6 and have a difference of 0·2?

$\boxed{0{\cdot}1}$ $\boxed{0{\cdot}3}$ $\boxed{0{\cdot}5}$ $\boxed{0{\cdot}2}$ $\boxed{0{\cdot}4}$

3 Here are some more pieces of track.

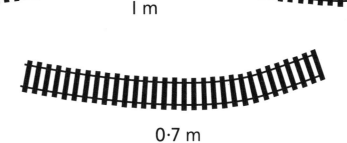

1 m

0·1 m

0·2 m

0·7 m

a) Isla puts the 0·1 m, 0·2 m and 0·7 m pieces of track together.

What mistake has Isla made?

The total length of my track is 0·10 m, because 1 + 2 + 7 = 10

Isla

b) Richard puts the 0·7 m and 1 m pieces of track together.

What is the difference between the two pieces?

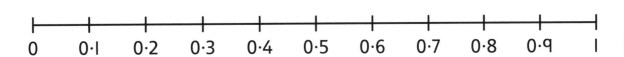

0	0·1	0·2	0·3	0·4	0·5	0·6	0·7	0·8	0·9	1

I used a number line and added on to find the difference.

I subtracted 0·7 m from 1 m.

11

Adding and subtracting decimals ②

Discover

① **a)** How much orange paint can Olivia and Luis make?

b) How much more orange paint do they need to make?

Share

I used column addition, just like when adding whole numbers.

a) Olivia and Luis can add 0·23 l of yellow paint to 0·45 l of red paint.

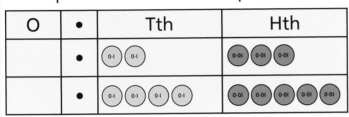

O	•	Tth	Hth
	•	0·1 0·1	0·01 0·01 0·01
	•	0·1 0·1 0·1 0·1	0·01 0·01 0·01 0·01 0·01

```
  O · Tth Hth
  0 ·  2   3
+ 0 ·  4   5
-----------
  0 ·  6   8
```

0·23 + 0·45 = 0·68   Olivia and Luis can make 0·68 l of orange paint.

b) A subtraction will show how much more orange paint they need to make.

O	•	Tth	Hth
		0·1 0·1 0·1 0·1 0·1	0·01 0·01 0·01 0·01 0·01
	•	0·1 0·1	0·01 0·01 0·01 0·01 0·01
			0·01 0·01 0·01 0·01 0·01

```
  O · Tth Hth
  0 ·  ⁶7̸  ¹5
− 0 ·  6   8
-----------
    ·      7
```

First, exchange 1 tenth for 10 hundredths. Then, subtract the hundredths.

O	•	Tth	Hth
		0·1 0·1 0·1 0·1 0·1	0·01 0·01 0·01 0·01 0·01
	•	0·1	0·01 0·01 0·01 0·01 0·01
			0·01 0·01 0·01 0·01 0·01

```
  O · Tth Hth
  0 ·  ⁶7̸  ¹5
− 0 ·  6   8
-----------
  0 ·  0   7
```

Subtract the tenths.

0·75 − 0·68 = 0·07 l

O	•	Tth	Hth
		0·1 0·1 0·1 0·1 0·1	0·01 0·01 0·01 0·01 0·01
	•	0·1	0·01 0·01 0·01 0·01 0·01
			0·01 0·01 0·01 0·01 0·01

```
  O · Tth Hth
  0 ·  ⁶7̸  ¹5
− 0 ·  6   8
-----------
  0 ·  0   7
```

Olivia and Luis need to make 0·07 l more orange paint.

Think together

1 **a)** Look at the containers. How much orange paint can be made?

yellow 0·41 l   red 0·42 l   orange

O	•	Tth	Hth
	•	0·1 0·1 0·1 0·1	0·01
	•	0·1 0·1 0·1 0·1	0·01 0·01

	O	·	Tth	Hth
	0	·	4	1
+	0	·	4	2
		·		

 ⬚ + ⬚ = ⬚ l

⬚ litres of orange paint can be made.

b) Bronwyn adds the water and the blackcurrant to make blackcurrant squash.

How much squash can be made?

0·29 l   0·22 l

O	•	Tth	Hth
	•	0·1 0·1	0·01 0·01 0·01 0·01 0·01 0·01 0·01 0·01 0·01
	•	0·1 0·1	0·01 0·01

	O	·	Tth	Hth
		·		
+		·		
		·		

I think I might need to do an exchange this time.

⬚ + ⬚ = ⬚ l

⬚ litres of squash can be made.

2 **a)** Jamilla has two tins of soup. How much soup does she have in total?

Jamilla has ⬚ l of soup in total.

b) She needs 1 litre of soup for all her friends for lunch. How much more does she need?

Jamilla needs ⬚ l more soup.

Soup 0.39 l

Soup 0.52 l

CHALLENGE

3 Kate and Ebo each have a bucket of slime.

My bucket has 0·27 l in it.

My bucket has 0·22 l more than yours in it.

Ebo

Kate

a) How much slime do they have altogether?

b) They need 1 litre of slime in total. How much more slime do they need?

To find 'altogether', I need to work out how much Kate has first.

I used a number line to work out how much more slime they needed.

15

Adding and subtracting decimals ❸

Discover

I need to decorate the other 2 sides of the mirror. Is there enough paper?

I m

I m

Aki

Ribbon I m

0·3 m   0·43 m   0·57 m   0·7 m

❶ **a)** How can Aki use the paper to decorate the other two sides of the mirror?

b) Aki bought I m of ribbon. He used 0·235 m to go around the outside of his treasure box.

How much ribbon does Aki have left?

Share

a) Aki has two 1 m sides of mirror to cover. He needs to find paper pieces that make 1 m.

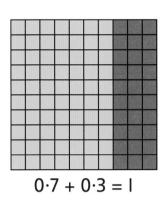

$$
\begin{array}{r}
\text{O}\ \cdot\ \text{Tth} \\
0\ \cdot\ 7 \\
+\ 0\ \cdot\ 3 \\
\hline
1\ \cdot\ 0 \\
{}^{1}
\end{array}
$$

0·7 + 0·3 = 1

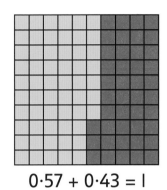

$$
\begin{array}{r}
\text{O}\ \cdot\ \text{Tth}\ \text{Hth} \\
0\ \cdot\ 5\quad 7 \\
+\ 0\ \cdot\ 4\quad 3 \\
\hline
1\ \cdot\ 0\quad 0 \\
{}^{1}\quad{}^{1}
\end{array}
$$

0·57 + 0·43 = 1

I remember! On a hundredths grid, 1 column is equal to 1 tenth (0·1) or 10 hundredths (0·10).

I used number bonds to 10 and 100 to work out which ones added to one whole.

Aki can use the 0·7 m and 0·3 m pieces to decorate one side of the mirror and 0·57 m and 0·43 m to decorate the other side.

b) We need to do a subtraction to work how much ribbon Aki has left.

I used number bonds to 1,000 to check my answer.

235 + 765 = 1,000

1 m ribbon

0·765 m	0·235 m

Write 1 as 1·000 and subtract 0·235.

Aki has 0·765 m of ribbon left.

$$
\begin{array}{r}
\text{O}\ \cdot\ \text{Tth}\ \ \text{Hth}\ \ \text{THth} \\
{}^{0}\cancel{1}\ \cdot\ {}^{9}\cancel{0}\ \ {}^{9}\cancel{0}\ \ {}^{1}0 \\
-\ 0\ \cdot\ 2\quad 3\quad 5 \\
\hline
0\ \cdot\ 7\quad 6\quad 5
\end{array}
$$

Think together

1 These pieces of decorative paper have been cut from I m strips of paper.

Find the amount left from each strip.

a)

0·4 m

I m − ⬜ m = ⬜ m

b)

0·49 m

I m − ⬜ m = ⬜ m

c)

0·68 m

I m − ⬜ m = ⬜ m

2 Write the missing numbers.

a)

1

0·2

b)

1

0·71

c)

1

0·132

d)

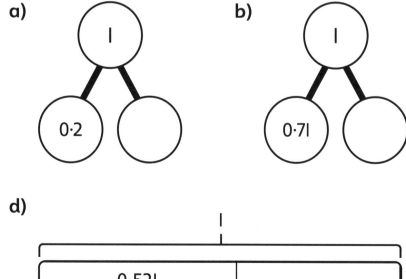

0·521

3 Look at the place value grids.

O	•	Tth	Hth
	•	0·1 0·1	0·01 0·01 0·01 0·01 0·01 0·01 0·01 0·01 0·01

O	•	Tth	Hth	Thth
	•	0·1 0·1 0·1 0·1 0·1 0·1 0·1	0·01 0·01	0·001 0·001 0·001 0·001

Use more counters to work out the missing numbers.

a) $0·29 + \boxed{} = 1$

b) $0·724 + \boxed{} = 1$

> For the first one, I think I need to add 1 hundredth and 8 tenths counters so there are 10 in each column. Then I can exchange.

> I do not think that is right. When you add a hundredth you need to do an exchange before you add some tenths.

c) Work out the missing numbers so that each calculation is true.

$0·34 + \boxed{} + 0·21 = 1$

$0·34 - 0·21 + \boxed{} = 1$

$0·234 + \boxed{} + \boxed{} = 1$

→ Practice book 5C p12

Adding and subtracting decimals ❹

Discover

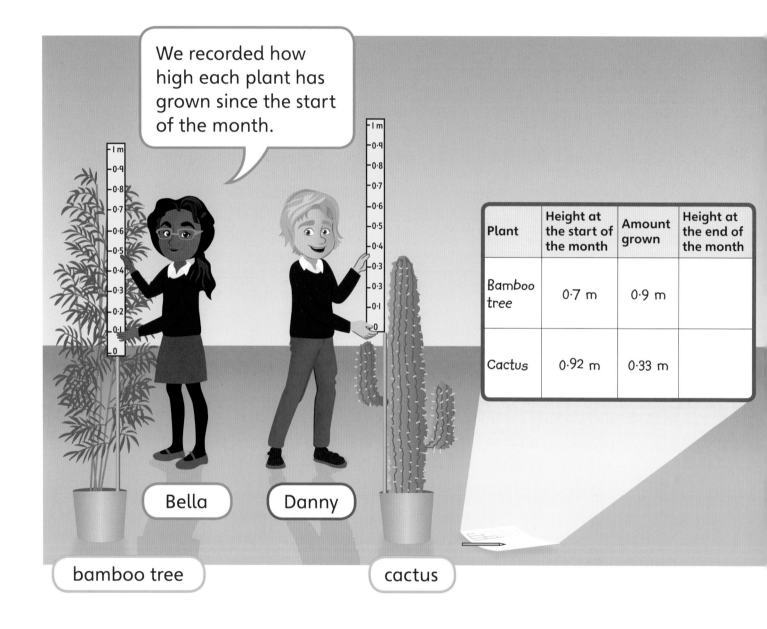

We recorded how high each plant has grown since the start of the month.

Bella

Danny

bamboo tree

cactus

Plant	Height at the start of the month	Amount grown	Height at the end of the month
Bamboo tree	0·7 m	0·9 m	
Cactus	0·92 m	0·33 m	

1 **a)** What is the height of each plant at the end of the month?

b) How much taller than the cactus is the bamboo tree?

Share

a) At the start of the month the bamboo tree was 0·7 m tall. It grows by 0·9 m. We need to add 0·7 and 0·9.

I used a number line to help me work out the height of the bamboo tree.

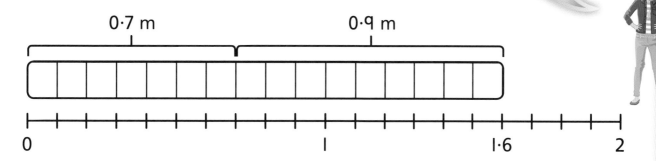

0·7 m   0·9 m

0   1   1·6   2

0·7 + 0·9 = 1·6. At the end of the month the height of the bamboo tree is 1·6 m.

The cactus is 0·92 m tall at the start of the month. It grows by 0·33 m.

We need to add 0·33 to 0·92.

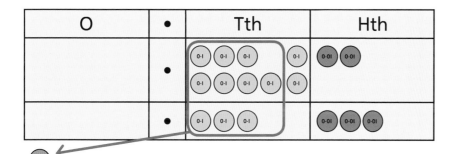

O	•	Tth	Hth
	•		
	•		
	•		

$$\begin{array}{r} \text{O} \cdot \text{Tth Hth} \\ 0 \cdot 9 \ 2 \\ + \ 0 \cdot 3 \ 3 \\ \hline 1 \cdot 2 \ 5 \\ {\scriptstyle 1} \end{array}$$

0·92 + 0·33 = 1·25

At the end of the month the height of the cactus is 1·25 m.

I used column addition to add 0·92 and 0·33.

When I added the tenths, I got 12 tenths. This is the same as 1 whole and 2 tenths.

b)

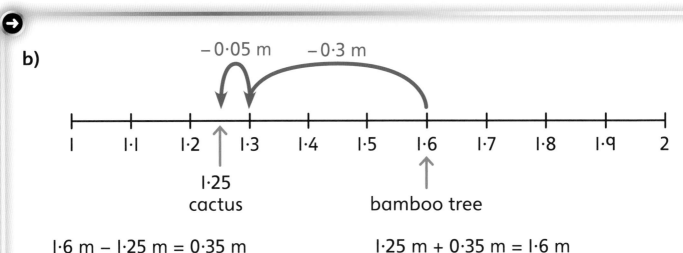

$1.6 \text{ m} - 1.25 \text{ m} = 0.35 \text{ m}$ $\qquad$ $1.25 \text{ m} + 0.35 \text{ m} = 1.6 \text{ m}$

The bamboo tree is 0·35 m taller than the cactus.

Think together

1 Bella and Danny also measured a sunflower.

What is the height of the sunflower at the end of the month?

Plant	Height at the start of the month	Amount grown	Height at the end of the month
Sunflower	0·67 m	0·75 m	

O	•	Tth	Hth
	•	0·1 0·1 0·1 0·1 0·1 / 0·1	0·01 0·01 0·01 0·01 0·01 / 0·01 0·01
	•	0·1 0·1 0·1 0·1 0·1 / 0·1 0·1	0·01 0·01 0·01 0·01 0·01

```
  O · Tth Hth
  0 · 6   7
+ 0 · 7   5
_____·_____
```

$0.67 + 0.75 = \boxed{}$

At the end of the month the height of the sunflower is $\boxed{}$ m.

2 **a)** Emma collects 0·5 kg of apples from her apple tree. She then collects 0·7 kg of plums.

I collected 0·12 kg of fruit in total.

Emma

Explain why Emma is wrong.

b) Max adds two numbers together.

What mistake has he made?

```
  O · Tth Hth
  0 ·  4   8
+ 0 ·  7   1
  0 ·  11  9
```

---

3 Find the missing numbers to make these calculations correct.

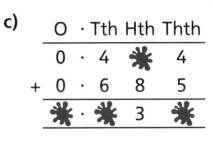
CHALLENGE

a)
```
  O · Tth
  0 · 8
+ 0 · ✹
  1 · 3
```

b)
```
  O · Tth Hth
  0 ·  ✹   2
+ 0 ·  3   ✹
  1 ·  2   7
```

c)
```
  O · Tth Hth Thth
  0 ·  4   ✹    4
+ 0 ·  6   8    5
  ✹ ·  ✹   3    ✹
```

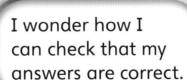

I wonder how I can check that my answers are correct.

23

Adding and subtracting decimals **5**

Discover

Menu
Pizza   £2·96
Juice   £1·04
...ghetti
...n & chips

I only have £4.

My meal costs £1·35 more than yours.

Max

Jamie

1 **a)** Max wants to buy a pizza and a juice. Does he have enough money?

   b) What is the total cost of Jamie's meal?

Share

a) Add £2·96 and £1·04 to work out the total cost of a pizza and a juice.

Add the hundredths first.

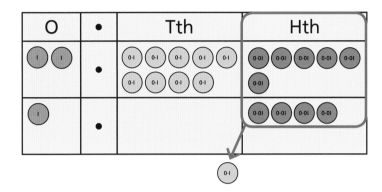

O	•	Tth	Hth
	2	· 9	6
+	1	· 0	4
		·	0
		1	

Add the tenths next.

O	•	Tth	Hth

O	·	Tth	Hth
	2	· 9	6
+	1	· 0	4
		· 0	0
	1	1	

Finally, add the Is.

O	•	Tth	Hth

O	·	Tth	Hth
	2	· 9	6
+	1	· 0	4
	4	· 0	0
		1	1

Max's meal costs £4 in total, so he has enough money.

I used the column method to add the two amounts.

b) Jamie's meal costs £1·35 more than Max's.

We need to work out £4 + £1·35.

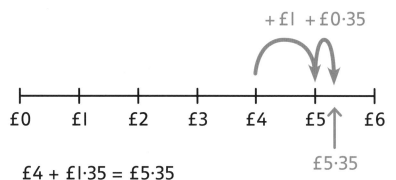

> I used a number line and added on the whole £s first and then the part of the whole.

£4 + £1·35 = £5·35

The total cost of Jamie's meal is £5·35.

Think together

1 Here are some items for sale in a supermarket.

| Bag of apples £1·99 | Bananas £2·34 | Melon £2·15 | Bag of pears £1·70 | Bag of cherries £3·57 |

How much do these items cost in total?

a) bananas and melon

```
  O · Tth Hth
  2 · 3   4
+ 2 · 1   5
─────────────
    ·
```

The total cost is £ ⬚.

b) pears and cherries

```
  O · Tth Hth
  1 · 7   0
+ 3 · 5   7
─────────────
    ·
```

The total cost is £ ⬚.

2 Work out the missing numbers.

a)

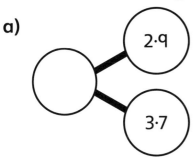

b)

2·453	5·232

c) 6 ones, 3 tenths and 4 hundredths plus 7 ones, 2 tenths and 9 hundredths is equal to ☐ tens, ☐ ones, ☐ tenths and ☐ hundredths.

3 Jamilla buys three items. She pays exactly £12.

CHALLENGE

a) Which items did she choose?

☐ + ☐ + ☐ = £12·00

> I am going to add the last digits and see if any add up to 0.

£0·94

£3·15

£2·38

£4·26

£6·47

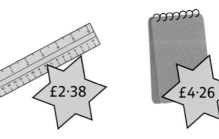

b) When added together, two of the items cost exactly the same as another two items.

Which items are they?

☐ + ☐ = ☐ + ☐

> I wonder how to check that my answers are correct.

27

Adding and subtracting decimals ❻

Discover

1 a) How much does the watermelon cost?

b) Amelia gives Toshi £6·00. How much change does she get?

Share

a) To find the cost of the watermelon we need to subtract £2·25 from £5·74.

£5·74	
£2·25	?

I am going to use a column method. I will start from the right-hand column.

Subtract the 5 hundredths first.

There are not enough hundredths.

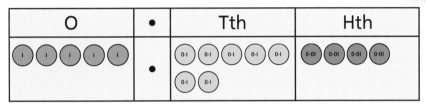

Exchange 1 tenth for 10 hundredths.

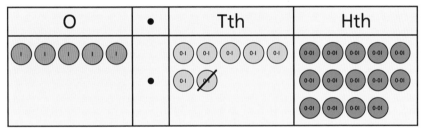

Now subtract the 5 hundredths.

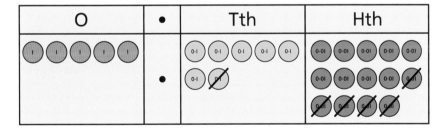

Now subtract the 2 tenths, then the 2 ones.

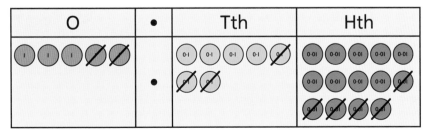

The watermelon costs £3·49.

b) To find the change we need to subtract.

£6·00 − £5·74 = ?

I used a number line to count on to find the difference. I think this is an efficient way to find change.

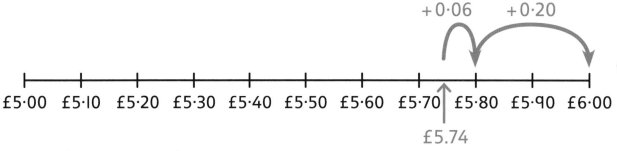

+0·06   +0·20

£5·00 £5·10 £5·20 £5·30 £5·40 £5·50 £5·60 £5·70 £5·80 £5·90 £6·00

£5.74

Amelia gets 26p change.

Think together

1 A shop sells some socks and hats.

How much cheaper is the hat than the socks?

£3·52   £5.15

O	•	Tth	Hth
① ① ① ① ①	•	0·1	0·01 0·01 0·01 0·01 0·01

$$
\begin{array}{r}
O \cdot \text{Tth} \ \text{Hth} \\
5 \cdot 1 \ \ 5 \\
- \ 3 \cdot 5 \ \ 2 \\
\hline
\cdot \\
\end{array}
$$

◻ − ◻ = ◻

The hat is £◻ cheaper than the socks.

2 Write these as column subtractions and complete them.

Predict how many exchanges you will need to make.

a) 37·5 − 13·9 = ☐

b) 2·654 − 1·375 = ☐

Did you predict correctly?

3 Lexi, Ebo and Reena are thinking of numbers.

Lexi

If I add 2·7 to my number I get 7·3.

I started with 12·65 and subtracted 3·92 to get to my number.

Ebo

Reena

If I add 1·23 to my number and then add 3·57, my answer is 12·04.

Ebo says that to work out Lexi's number you need to subtract. He does the following calculation.

a) What mistake has Ebo made?

b) What are Ebo and Reena's numbers?

```
  O · Tth
  7 · 3
− 2 · 7
  5 · 4
```

I wonder why I have to subtract to find Lexi's number.

I think it is because you have to do the inverse since Lexi has already added on 2·7 to get 7·3.

→ Practice book 5C p21

Adding and subtracting decimals 7

Discover

My paper plane flew 4·23 m.

My plane flew 1·6 m farther than yours.

Andy

Ambika

Lee

1 a) How far did Ambika's paper plane fly?

b) Lee throws his paper plane. It flies the shortest distance at 0·42 m less than Andy's plane. How far does Lee's paper plane fly?

Share

a) Andy's plane flew 4·23 m. Ambika's plane flew 1·6 m farther.

We need to add 4·23 and 1·6.

O	•	Tth	Hth
① ① ① ①	•	0·1 0·1	0·01 0·01 0·01

$$
\begin{array}{r}
\text{O} \cdot \text{Tth Hth} \\
4 \cdot 2 \ 3 \\
+ \ 1 \cdot 6 \ 0 \\
\hline
5 \cdot 8 \ 3 \\
\end{array}
$$

4·23 + 1·6 = 5·83

Ambika's paper plane flew 5·83 m.

> I used the column method to add. I lined the numbers up at the decimal point. I added an extra 0 in the hundredths column to make the same number of digits after the decimal point.

b) Lee's plane flies 0·42 m less than Andy's plane.

Method 1

$$
\begin{array}{r}
\text{O} \cdot \text{Tth Hth} \\
^3\cancel{4} \cdot {}^1 2 \ 3 \\
- \ 0 \cdot 4 \ 2 \\
\hline
3 \cdot 8 \ 1 \\
\end{array}
$$

Method 2

4·23 m = 423 cm

0·42 m = 42 cm

423 − 42 = 381 cm = 3·81 m

> I converted all the measurements into centimetres and then subtracted.

Lee's paper plane flies 3·81 m.

Think together

1 More of the class took part in the paper plane throwing competition.

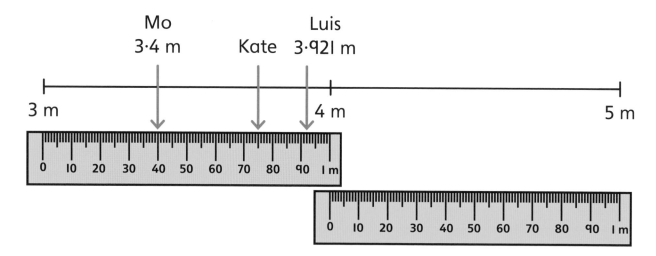

a) Mo had a second throw. He threw 0·65 m farther than his first throw. How far did his second throw fly?

O	•	Tth	Hth
①①①	•	⁰·¹ ⁰·¹ ⁰·¹ ⁰·¹	

3·4 + 0·65 = ☐

Mo's second throw flew ☐ m.

```
  O · Tth Hth
  3 · 4   0
+ 0 · 6   5
_____
    ·
```

b) How much farther than Kate's plane did Luis's plane fly?

O	•	Tth	Hth	Thth
①①①	•	⁰·¹ ⁰·¹ ⁰·¹ ⁰·¹ ⁰·¹ ⁰·¹ ⁰·¹ ⁰·¹ ⁰·¹	⁰·⁰¹ ⁰·⁰¹	⁰·⁰⁰¹

☐ – ☐ = ☐

```
  O · Tth Hth Thth
  3 · 9   2   1
− 3 · 7   5   0
_____
    ·
```

2 Complete this addition pyramid.

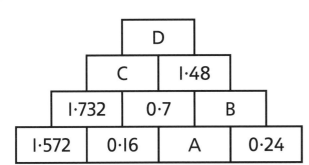

Pyramid:
- Top: D
- C | 1·48
- 1·732 | 0·7 | B
- 1·572 | 0·16 | A | 0·24

A = ☐
B = ☐
C = ☐
D = ☐

Remember, in an addition pyramid each pair of numbers adds up to the number above it.

CHALLENGE

3 **a)** What mistakes have been made in these calculations?

| 4·5 + 1·34 | | 8·2 − 1·86 | | 82·43 − 1·89 |

O	·	Tth	Hth
	4	·	5
+ 1	·	3	4
1	·	7	9

O	·	Tth	Hth
8	·	2	0
− 1	·	8	6
7	·	6	6

T	O	·	Tth	Hth
8	2	·	¹4	¹3
	− 1	·	8	9
8	1	·	6	4

b) What does the correct working out look like?

I think some of these calculations have been lined up incorrectly.

Maybe I could do calculations to check my answers.

35

→ Practice book 5C p24

Adding and subtracting decimals 8

Discover

1. **a)** How much juice is in the two bottles in total?

   b) Jamilla started with a full bag of flour. How much is left in the bag now some flour is on the scales?

Share

I did a column addition.

a) There is one 5 l bottle and one 1·25 l bottle of juice.

O	•	Tth	Hth

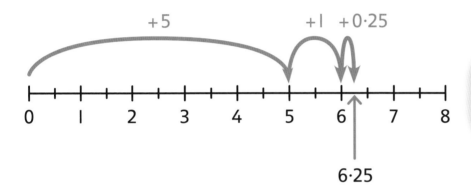

$$
\begin{array}{r}
\ \ 5 \cdot 0\ \ 0 \\
+\ \ 1 \cdot 2\ \ 5 \\
\hline
\ \ 6 \cdot 2\ \ 5 \\
\end{array}
$$

I added the wholes and then added the part.

6·25

There are 6·25 l of juice in the two bottles in total.

b) The full bag of flour weighed 2 kg. Jamilla tipped 0·296 kg onto the scales.

The amount of flour left in the bag is 2 − 0·296.

O	•	Tth	Hth	Thth

$$
\begin{array}{r}
{}^{1}\cancel{2} \cdot {}^{9}\cancel{0}\ {}^{9}\cancel{0}\ {}^{1}0 \\
-\ 0 \cdot 2\ \ 9\ \ 6 \\
\hline
1 \cdot 7\ \ 0\ \ 4 \\
\end{array}
$$

2 kg − 0·296 kg = 1·704 kg.

There is 1·704 kg of flour left in the bag.

Remember that 2 can be written as 2·000 so that there are the same number of digits after the decimal.

37

Think together

1 **a)** How much pasta is there in total?

O	•	Tth
① ① ① ① ①	•	
① ①	•	0·1 0·1 0·1 0·1 0·1
		0·1 0·1 0·1

$$\begin{array}{r} O \cdot Tth \\ 5 \cdot 0 \\ + 2 \cdot 8 \\ \hline \cdot \\ \hline \end{array}$$

There is ☐ kg of pasta in total.

b) What is the total mass of the cereal?

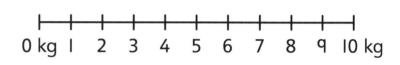

0 kg 1 2 3 4 5 6 7 8 9 10 kg

There is ☐ kg of cereal in total.

c) Zac pours some milk from the bottle into a glass.
The glass holds 0·35 l of milk.

O	•	Tth	Hth
① ① ⊘	•	0·1 0·1 0·1 0·1 0·1	0·01 0·01 0·01 0·01 0·01
	•	0·1 0·1 0·1 0·1 ⊘	0·01 0·01 0·01 0·01 0·01

$$\begin{array}{r} O \cdot Tth\ Hth \\ 3 \cdot 0\ \ 0 \\ - 0 \cdot 3\ \ 5 \\ \hline \cdot \\ \hline \end{array}$$

How much milk is left in the bottle?

☐ l are left in the bottle.

2 Work out which weights are on the weighing scales.

CHALLENGE

3 Jamilla uses two different methods to work out 2 − 0·296.

Method I

O	·	Tth	Hth	Thth
1	·	9	9	9
− 0	·	2	9	6
1	·	7	0	3

1·703 + 0·001 = 1·704

Method 2

O	·	Tth	Hth	Thth
1	·	9	9	9
− 0	·	2	9	5
1	·	7	0	4

1·999 − 0·295 = 1·704

a) Why do Jamilla's methods work? Which method do you prefer?

> This makes the subtraction easier. I wonder why it shows the same answer as 2 − 0·296 though.

> I could use a number line to prove that 2 − 0·296 is the same as 1·999 − 0·295.

b) Use your preferred method to work these calculations out.

| 6 − 3·45 | 3 − 0·914 | 26 − 2·8 |

39

Decimal sequences

Discover

These rose bushes grow 2·5 cm every month.

Mo

Olivia

1 **a)** The rose bush Mo and Olivia are planting is 15·4 cm tall in April. How tall will it be each coming month for the next 6 months?

b) The other rose bush is 87·2 cm. For how many months has the rose bush been over 60 cm tall?

Share

a) The rose bush starts at 15·4 cm and grows 2·5 cm each month. Add on 2·5 cm to its height from the previous month.

I made a table to organise the results. I also showed the same sequence on a number line.

Month	April	May	June	July	Aug	Sept	Oct
Height (cm)	15·4	17·9	20·4	22·9	25·4	27·9	30·4

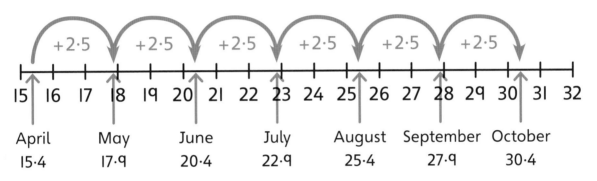

April	May	June	July	August	September	October
15·4	17·9	20·4	22·9	25·4	27·9	30·4

The rule is to add 2·5 each time.

These numbers are in a sequence. A sequence is when related things happen in an order. This sequence goes up by the same amount each time.

b) Subtract 2·5 each time, until we get less than 60.

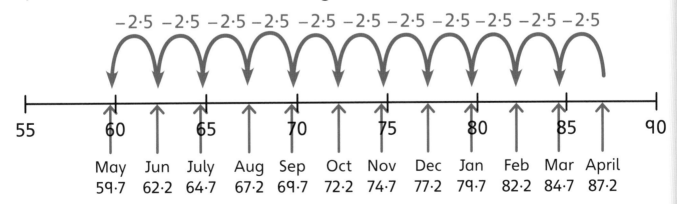

	May	Jun	July	Aug	Sep	Oct	Nov	Dec	Jan	Feb	Mar	April
	59·7	62·2	64·7	67·2	69·7	72·2	74·7	77·2	79·7	82·2	84·7	87·2

11 months ago, the rose bush was shorter than 60 cm. So, the rose bush has been over 60 cm tall for the last 10 months.

41

Think together

I wonder how to find the rule. Maybe I can look at how much each rose has grown by each month.

1 The heights of the roses each month make a sequence.

All the heights are in cm.

Find the rules and complete the missing numbers.

	April	May	June	July	Aug	Sept	Oct
White rose	15·1	15·2	15·3	☐	☐	☐	☐
Climbing rose	10·0	12·6	☐	☐	☐	☐	☐
Wild rose	☐	12·43	12·431	12·432	☐	☐	☐

2 Work out the sequences and complete the missing values.

a)

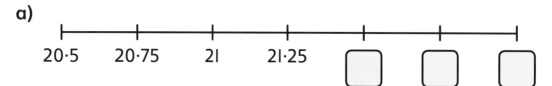

20·5   20·75   21   21·25   ☐   ☐   ☐

b)

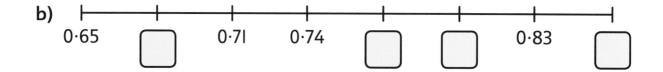

0·65   ☐   0·71   0·74   ☐   ☐   0·83   ☐

c)

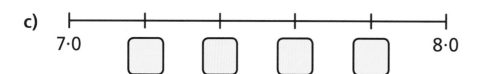

7·0   ☐   ☐   ☐   ☐   8·0

CHALLENGE

3 These decimal cards form a sequence when arranged in ascending order.

Two of the cards in each sequence are covered up. What could they be?

Describe to a partner the pattern that these decimals make.

a)

| 3·7 | 3·5 | 3·9 | 4·0 |  |

I am going to put the cards in order and try and work out what they go up in.

To find what they go up in, I will do a subtraction.

b)

| 35·6 | 38·7 | 32·5 | 41·8 | 29·4 | 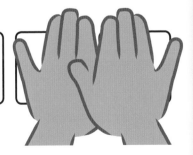 |

c) What would be the first number above 50 in the second sequence?

43

Problem solving – decimals ❶

Discover

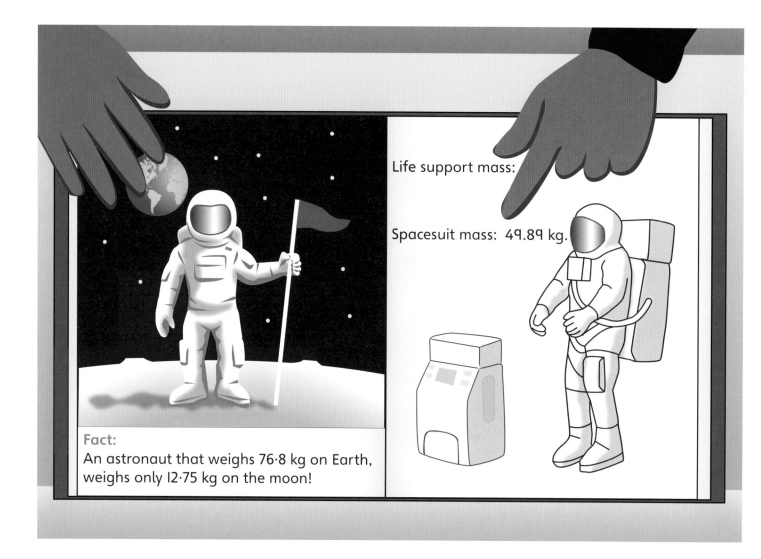

Life support mass:

Spacesuit mass: 49.89 kg.

Fact:
An astronaut that weighs 76·8 kg on Earth, weighs only 12·75 kg on the moon!

❶ **a)** How much more is the weight of the astronaut on Earth than on the moon?

b) The mass of the life support is 90·2 kg heavier than the spacesuit.

What is the total mass of the spacesuit and life support?

Share

a) moon

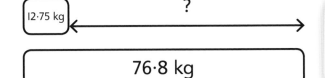

12·75 kg   ?

Earth   76·8 kg

> I will use a bar model to help me. I can see that I need to do a subtraction as I am finding a difference.

```
   T   O  ·  Tth  Hth
   7   6  ·  ⁷8̸  ¹0
 - 1   2  ·  7    5
   6   4  ·  0    5
```

76·8 − 12·75 = 64·05

The weight of the astronaut on Earth is 64·05 kg more than on the moon.

b) spacesuit   49.89

life support   90.2   ?

> I need to find the mass of the life support first.

The mass of the life support is

49·89 kg + 90·2 kg = 140·09 kg.

The total mass of the spacesuit and the life support is

140·09 kg + 49·89 kg = 189·98 kg.

```
    H   T   O  ·  Tth  Hth
        9   0  ·  2    0
  +     4   9  ·  8    9
    1   4   0  ·  0    9
            ₁       ₁
```

```
    H   T   O  ·  Tth  Hth
    1   4   0  ·  0    9
  +     4   9  ·  8    9
    1   8   9  ·  9    8
                ₁
```

The total mass of the spacesuit and the life support is 189·98 kg.

Think together

1 Lexi can jump up to 1·5 m on Earth. The same jump would be 9·144 m on the moon because the gravity is different.

How much farther could Lexi jump on the moon?

Earth | 1·5 m |

?

moon | 9·144 m |

O	·	Tth	Hth	Thth
9	·	1	4	4
− 1	·	5		
	·			

Lexi could jump ⬜ m farther on the moon.

2 How much do the science magazines cost in total?

Explain your method.

SCIENCE £4·99   SCIENCE £2·99   SCIENCE £5·88

?

| £4·99 | £2·99 | £5·88 |

3 Astronauts bring three rocks back from the moon.

CHALLENGE

Rock A

Rock B
12 kg

Rock C

The mass of rock A is 3·6 kg less than rock B.

The mass of rock C is 4·75 kg greater than rock B.

a) Work out the total mass of the three rocks.

b) How much more does rock C weigh than rock A?

I am going to work out the mass of each of the rocks.

I am not sure that you need to. There might be a more efficient way. A bar model will help work it out.

47

Problem solving – decimals ❷

Discover

① **a)** What will happen to the balance scale when Ebo puts the bag of sugar in the empty balance pan?

b) By adding or removing some sugar or oats to or from the bags, how can Emma and Ebo get the scales to balance?

Share

a) First, find the mass of the oats.

I will work out the mass of the pears and oats altogether.

Oats

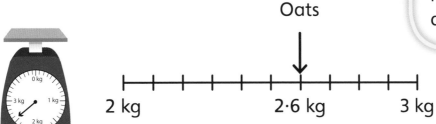

2 kg   2·6 kg   3 kg

The mass of the oats is 2·6 kg.

	O	·	Tth	Hth
	2	·	6	0
+	0	·	8	9
	3	·	4	9

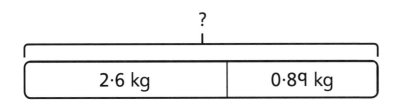

?

2·6 kg	0·89 kg

2·6 kg + 0·89 kg = 3·49 kg

3·49 kg > 3 kg, so the balance scale will not move. The sugar bag is not heavy enough to tip the balance.

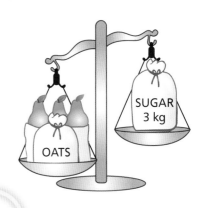

b)

To balance, the scales need to be the same mass either side. So, I need to either reduce the amount of oats or add more sugar.

3·49 − 3 = 0·49

Emma and Ebo can add 0·49 kg of sugar to the bag of sugar.

	O	·	Tth	Hth
	3	·	4	9
−	3	·	0	0
	0	·	4	9

Or they can remove 0·49 kg of oats from the bag of oats.

Think together

1 Emma weighs out some sugar from the 3 kg bag.

How much sugar is left in the bag?

> I think there is more than one way to work this out.

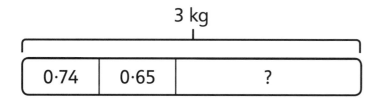

There is ☐ kg of sugar left in the bag.

2 A tablespoon holds 18·6 g of flour. A teaspoon holds 15·9 g less flour than the tablespoon.

What is the total mass of flour on the two spoons?

The total mass of flour on the two spoons is ☐ g.

3 A street has four lamp posts in a line. Jen measures the distances between some of the lamp posts.

CHALLENGE

> The distance between the 1st and 2nd lamp posts is 5·85 m. Between the 2nd and 3rd it is 6·189 m. The distance between the 1st and 4th lamp posts is 3 times the distance between the 1st and 2nd.

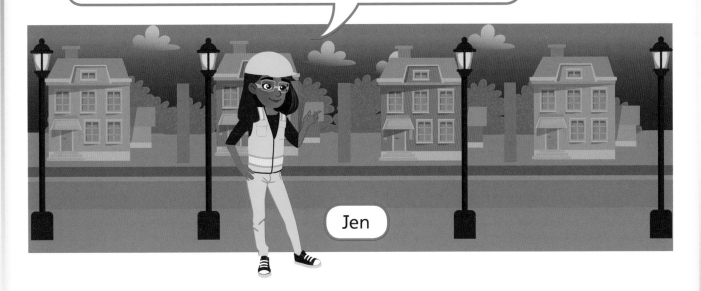

Jen

What is the distance between the 3rd and 4th lamp posts?

> I think I need to multiply decimals.

> I do not think you have to. I think you can add the number three times instead.

51

Multiplying decimals by 10

Discover

1 a) What is the answer to Kate and Richard's multiplication?

b) What mistake has Aki made?

What is the correct answer to Reena and Aki's multiplication?

Share

I used counters in a place value grid. I had to exchange.

a) Kate and Richard need to multiply 0·1 by 10.

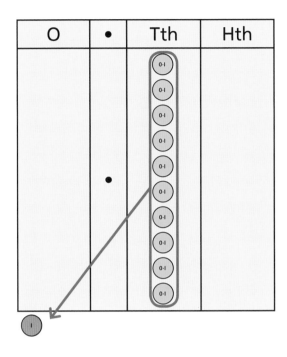

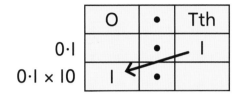

Place ten 0·1 counters in the tenths column.

Exchange ten 0·1 counters for one 1 counter.

0·1 × 10 = 1

The answer to Kate and Richard's multiplication is 1.

b) Aki thinks when you multiply by 10 you add a 0 to the end because this is what it looks like happens when you multiply a whole number by 10. This is incorrect.

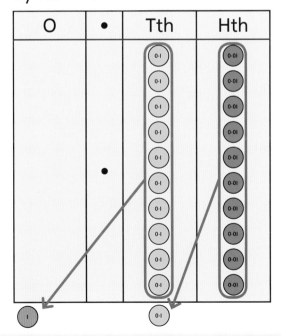

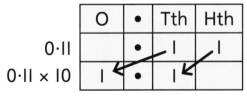

0·11 × 10 = 1·1

The correct answer to Reena and Aki's multiplication is 1·1.

We can write 1·1 instead of 1·10.

53

Think together

1 Use the counters and a place value grid to work out these multiplications.

a) $0.14 \times 10 = \boxed{}$

b) $2.3 \times 10 = \boxed{}$

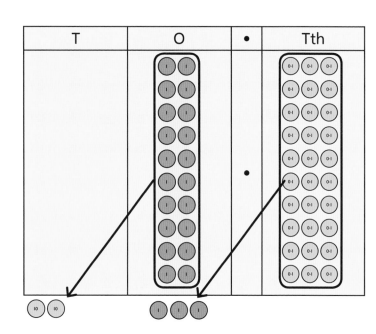

2 Multiply each of these numbers by 10.

a)

T	O	•	Tth	Hth
	3	•	7	
		•		

c)

T	O	•	Tth	Hth
	2	•	3	9
		•		

b)

T	O	•	Tth	Hth
	4	•	5	
		•		

d)

T	O	•	Tth	Hth	Thth
	0	•	1	9	6
		•			

3 Complete the multiplications.

a) $0{\cdot}1 \times 10 = \boxed{}$

$1{\cdot}2 \times 10 = \boxed{}$

$5{\cdot}7 \times 10 = \boxed{}$

$19{\cdot}1 \times 10 = \boxed{}$

b) $0{\cdot}72 \times 10 = \boxed{}$

$1{\cdot}25 \times 10 = \boxed{}$

$5{\cdot}71 \times 10 = \boxed{}$

$19{\cdot}16 \times 10 = \boxed{}$

c) $0{\cdot}256 \times 10 = \boxed{}$

$1{\cdot}256 \times 10 = \boxed{}$

$31{\cdot}126 \times 10 = \boxed{}$

d) With a partner, look at the digits in each number that is being multiplied by 10.

What do you notice about the digits in the answers?
What is the same and what is different?

4 Find the missing numbers in these multiplications.

a) $10 \times 3{\cdot}9 = \boxed{}$

b) $10 \times 11{\cdot}6 = \boxed{}$

c) $\boxed{} \times 10 = 4{\cdot}56$

d) $\boxed{} \times 10 = 12{\cdot}62$

e) $\boxed{} \times 10 = 3{\cdot}2$

f) $\boxed{} \times 10 = 15{\cdot}86$

CHALLENGE

I can multiply numbers by 10 without using counters and a place value grid.

I notice that when I multiply by 10, the digits move 1 place to the left. I wonder if this always happens.

55

→ Practice book 5C p39

Multiplying decimals by 10, 100 and 1,000

Discover

1 **a)** How many 2·5 kg bags of potatoes are on a pallet?

What is the total mass of all the bags on one pallet?

b) What is the mass of all the potatoes on the lorry?

Share

a) A bag contains 2·5 kg of potatoes. There are 10 bags in a sack.

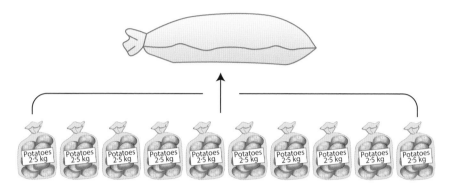

T	O	•	Tth	Hth
	2	•	5	
2	5	•		

2·5 × 10 = 25 kg. The mass of each sack is 25 kg.

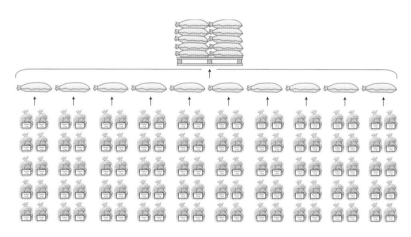

There are 10 sacks of potatoes on each pallet.

There are 10 bags in each sack.

10 × 10 = 100

There are 100 2·5 kg bags on a pallet.

We need to put a 0 to keep the place value of the number.

The total mass of all the bags on one pallet is 250 kg.

H	T	O	•	Tth
		2	•	5
2	5	0	•	

I multiplied by 10 as there are 10 bags in a sack. I then multiplied by 10 again as there are 10 sacks on a pallet. This is the same as multiplying by 100.

b) There are 10 pallets on the lorry.

$2·5 × 10 = 25$

$2·5 × 100 = 250$

$2·5 × 1,000 = 2,500$

Th	H	T	O	•	Tth
			2	•	5
		2	5	•	
	2	5	0	•	
2	5	0	0	•	

When multiplying by 100, the digits move two places to the left. When multiplying by 1,000, the digits move three places to the left.

Multiplying by 1,000 is the same as multiplying by 10, then 10 and then 10 again.

So $2·5 × 1,000$ is the same as $2·5 × 10 × 10 × 10 = 2,500$ kg. The mass of all the potatoes on the lorry is 2,500 kg.

Think together

1. Draw a place value grid and find the answers.

Th	H	T	O	•	Tth
			3	•	7
				•	
				•	
				•	

$3·7 × 10 = \boxed{}$

$3·7 × 100 = \boxed{}$

$3·7 × 1,000 = \boxed{}$

2 Use a place value grid to help you complete the multiplications.

Th	H	T	O	•	Tth	Hth	Thth
				•			
				•			
				•			

a) 1·72 × 10 = ☐

1·72 × 100 = ☐

1·72 × 1,000 = ☐

b) 4·13 × 1,000 = ☐

0·413 × 1,000 = ☐

0·041 × 1,000 = ☐

c) 39·3 × 100 = ☐

3·93 × 100 = ☐

0·393 × 100 = ☐

3 Can you find an efficient method to work out the answers?

Explain your method.

CHALLENGE

0·12 × 100   7·35 × 100   16·9 × 100   0·384 × 100

0·12 × 1,000   7·35 × 1,000   16·9 × 1,000   0·384 × 1,000

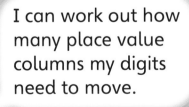
I can work out how many place value columns my digits need to move.

I notice that when I multiply by 100, I always move the digits the same number of places.

59

→ Practice book 5C p42

Dividing decimals by 10

Discover

1 a) What is the width of one of Danny's handspans in metres?

b) In metres, how much narrower is Lexi's handspan than Danny's?

Share

I need to divide each number by 10 to work out the width of each handspan.

a) Ten of Danny's handspans are 1·5 m long.

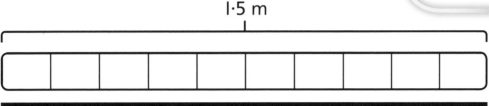

1·5 m

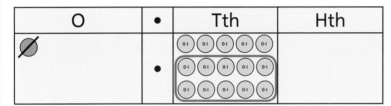

O	•	Tth	Hth
①	•	0·1 0·1 0·1 0·1 0·1	

Share 1·5 into 10 equal groups.

We share one 1 counter by exchanging it for ten 0·1 counters.

O	•	Tth	Hth
⊘	•	0·1 0·1 0·1 0·1 0·1	
	•	0·1 0·1 0·1 0·1 0·1 0·1 0·1 0·1 0·1 0·1	

If we divide 15 by 10 we get 1 and 5 left over.

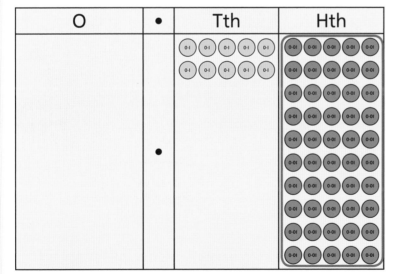

O	•	Tth	Hth

We need to exchange these for fifty 0·01 counters.

If we divide 50 by 10 we get 5.

So 1·5 ÷ 10 = 0·15

The width of one of Danny's handspans is 0·15 m.

O	•	Tth	Hth	THth
1	•	5		
0	•	1	5	

I notice that when I divide by 10, the digits move one place to the right.

b) Ten of Lexi's handspans are 0·9 metres wide in total.

$0·9 ÷ 10 = 0·09$

One of Lexi's handspans is 0·09 m wide.

$0·15 − 0·09 = 0·06$

Lexi's handspan is 0·06 m narrower than Danny's.

O	•	Tth	Hth
0	•	9	
0	•	0	9

I worked out the difference of the 10 handspans first and got 0·6. Then I divided 0·6 by 10.

The zeros are important as they ensure the other digits are in the correct columns.

Think together

1 Toshi makes a line of 10 footsteps.

2·6 metres

How long is each of Toshi's footsteps in metres?

O	•	Tth	Hth
① ①	•	0·1 0·1 0·1 0·1 0·1 0·1	

O	•	Tth	Hth
2	•	6	
	•		

Each of Toshi's footsteps is ☐ m.

2 Work out the missing numbers.

H	T	O	•	Tth	Hth	Thth
			•			
			•			

a) $0.92 \div 10 = \boxed{}$

b) $53.6 \div 10 = \boxed{}$

c) $95 \div 10 = \boxed{}$

d) $\boxed{} \div 10 = 5.86$

e) $89.02 \div 10 = \boxed{}$

f) $\boxed{} \div 10 = 1.002$

3 Use the pictures to answer the questions.

CHALLENGE

£1.20 1 l MILK

0.7 l — Squash 2.25 l — Water

Rice 5 kg   Rice 5 kg   Rice 4 kg   Rice 2 kg

a) Danny mixes the water and squash.
He shares it equally between 10 glasses.

How much drink is in each glass?

b) How much does 100 ml of milk cost?
What about 200 ml?

c) The rice is shared between 20 saucepans.

How much rice is in each saucepan?

I know there are 10 equal parts of 100 ml in 1 litre.

I think I can put half the rice in 10 pans and work it out from there.

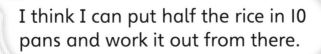

→ Practice book 5C p45

Dividing decimals by 10, 100 and 1,000

Discover

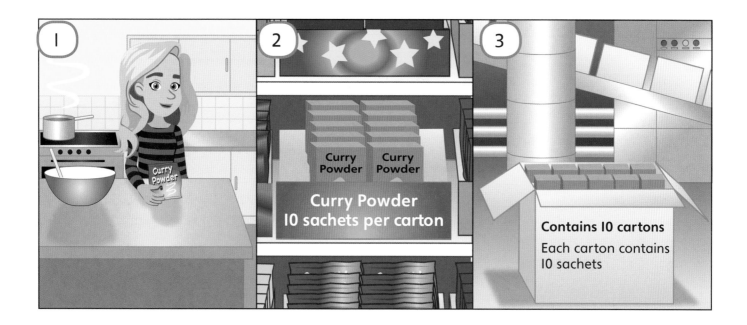

1 **a)** How many sachets of curry powder are in the large box?

b) The total mass of the curry power in the large box is 8·5 kg.

How many kilograms of curry powder is in each sachet?

Share

a) There are 10 sachets in each carton. There are 10 cartons in each large box.

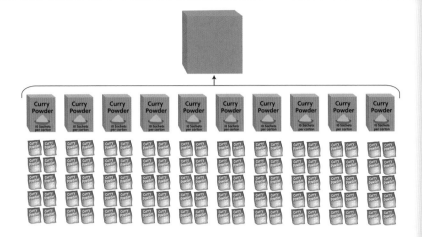

$10 \times 10 = 100$

There are 100 sachets of curry powder in the large box.

b) The total mass of the large box is 8·5 kg.

Method I

> I divided by 10 to work out how much is in each carton.

8·5

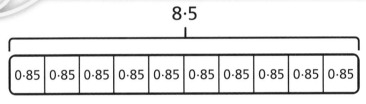

O	•	Tth	Hth	Thth
8	•	5		
0	•	8	5	

$8·5 \div 10 = 0·85$

> I divided by 10 again to work out how much curry is in each sachet.

0·85

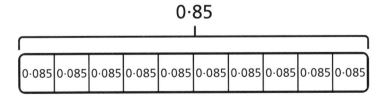

O	•	Tth	Hth	Thth
0	•	8	5	
0	•	0	8	5

$0·85 \div 10 = 0·085$

There is 0·085 kg of curry powder in each sachet.

Method 2

I divided by 100 instead as there are 100 sachets in the large box.

O	•	Tth	Hth	Thth
8	•	5		
0	•	0	→8	→5

When dividing by 100, the digits move 2 places to the right.

Dividing by 100 is the same as dividing by 10 and 10 again.

There is 0·085 kg of curry powder in each sachet.

Think together

1 Divide each of these numbers or amounts by 100.

H	T	O	•	Tth	Hth	Thth
			•			
			•			

12·8 kg ÷ 100 = ☐   128 ÷ 100 = ☐

2·52 m ÷ 100 = ☐   0.9 ÷ 100 = ☐

2 The milk is used in a recipe for 100 scones.

How much milk is in each scone?

☐ ÷ ☐ = ☐

There is ☐ l of milk in each scone.

4 l
MILK

3 Divide each of these numbers or amounts by 1,000.

a) 12   b) 6·2   c) 718 km   d) 0·7

4 In a bakery there is a trolley that holds 10 trays.

Each tray contains 10 loaves of bread.

Each loaf of bread is cut into 10 equal slices.

CHALLENGE

 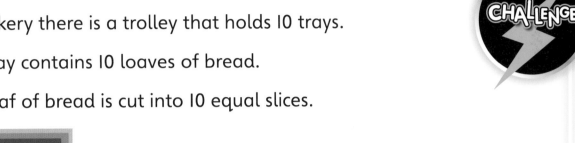 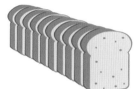

a) If the total mass of all the bread on a trolley is 46 kg, how much does a single slice weigh?

Explain your method.

b) What rule can you think of to show your method?

I will work out the number of slices and then divide the amount by this.

I will work out the mass of the loaves on a tray, then the mass of each loaf and then the mass of each slice.

67

→ Practice book 5C p48

End of unit check

1 What is the answer when these two numbers are added together?

| 2·53 | | 3·64 |

A 5·17   B 5·117   C 6·17   D 6·67

2 What is 0·35 subtracted from 15·6?

A 12·1   B 15·25   C 15·35   D 15·95

3 Which of the following is **not** equivalent to 5 − 3·45?

A 6 − 4·45   B 4·99 − 3·46   C 4·99 − 3·44   D 4·98 − 3·43

4 What is the answer to 0·2 × 100?

A 0·02   B 0·2   C 2   D 20

5 Which of these calculations is equal to 0·015?

A 15 ÷ 1,000   B 0·15 × 10   C 1·5 ÷ 10   D 15 × 100

6 Which statement is false?

   A When you multiply by 10, the digits move 1 place to the left.

   B When you multiply by 100, the digits move 2 places to the right.

   C When you divide by 10, the digits move 1 place to the right.

   D When you divide by 1,000, the digits move 3 places to the right.

7 A tube contains two tennis balls.

Each tennis balls weighs 0·16 kg.

The total mass of the tube and two balls is 0·5 kg.

What is the mass of the empty tube?

8 A, B and C are plotted on a number line.

The difference between A and B is 3·5.

The difference between A and C is 10 times the difference between A and B.

What are the values of B and C?

→ Practice book 5C p51

Unit 13
Geometry – properties of shapes ①

In this unit we will …

- ⚡ Measure angles in degrees
- ⚡ Learn to measure angles with a protractor
- ⚡ Draw lines and angles accurately
- ⚡ Calculate missing angles
- ⚡ Learn about angles in shapes

Do you remember about measuring angles as turns?

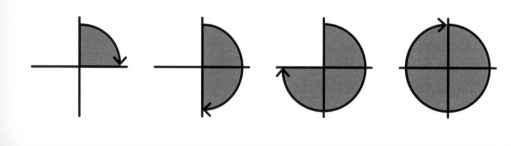

We will need some maths words. Which one can mean an angle that is a quarter turn?

angle   whole turn   right angle

acute angle   obtuse angle   reflex angle

degrees (°)   interior angle

clockwise   anticlockwise   orientation

We will need this too! Can you see where the mark for 55 mm is?

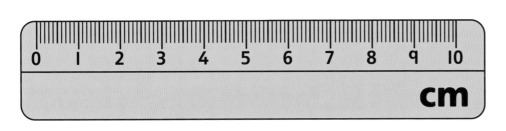

Measuring angles in degrees

Discover

1 a) Who will Lexi be facing after a 180-degree turn?

  b) Lexi tries a 90-degree turn. What could she be facing now?

Share

a) A 360-degree turn is a whole turn.

A 180-degree turn is a half turn.

> We measure turns in **degrees**. The ° symbol means degrees.

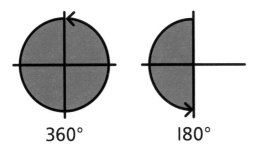

360°   180°

Lexi starts facing Reena.

After a 180-degree turn Lexi will be facing Lee.

b) A 90-degree turn is a quarter turn.

anticlockwise

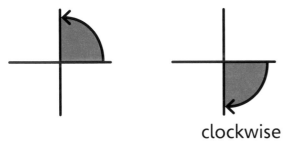

clockwise

This is also called a right angle.

Lexi starts facing Lee.

Lexi could turn 90° clockwise or 90° anticlockwise. She could be facing the flowers or the bench now.

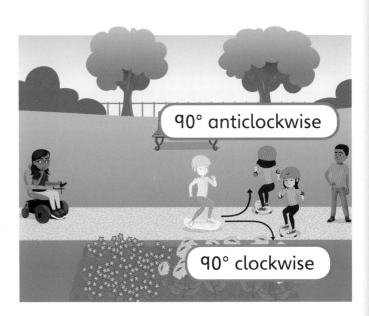

90° anticlockwise

90° clockwise

Think together

1 Lexi starts facing Lee. She makes four 90-degree turns clockwise. How many degrees has she turned? What or who is she facing now?

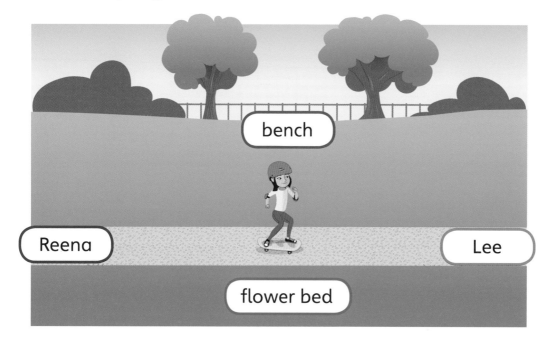

Lexi has turned ⬜° clockwise and she is now facing _____ .

2 Amelia is setting up the gym. She starts facing the bibs. She makes an anticlockwise turn and is now facing the gym mats.

How many degrees has she turned?

Amelia has turned ⬜°.

3 **a)** Mo is standing in the centre of points A to H.

Complete the table to describe which points he faces as he turns.

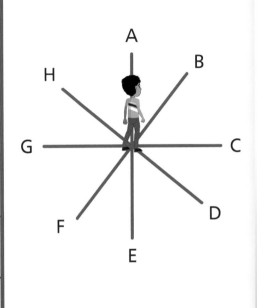

Start	Turn	Finish
facing B	180°	facing ☐
facing A	90° anticlockwise	facing ☐
facing E	☐° _____	facing C
facing G	☐° _____	facing A
facing G	☐° _____	facing H
facing ☐	45° clockwise	facing B

b) Mo faces G. Then he turns to face B.

Describe two different turns he could have made.

I will work out how many degrees there are in one part of the turn.

I think he could turn clockwise or anticlockwise.

→ Practice book 5C p54

Measuring with a protractor ❶

Discover

Amal

Holly

❶ **a)** Amal and Holly are using a ramp to test the grip of some new trainers. What angle is the ramp at now?

b) Amal records the angle as 150°. Explain his mistake.

Share

a) You can use a protractor to measure angles.

Step I

Make sure the zero line of the protractor matches the start of the angle turn.

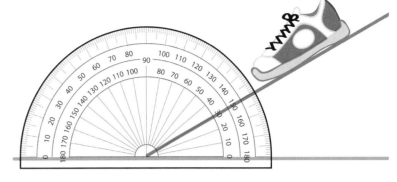

Step 2

Line up the centre mark with the exact point of the angle.

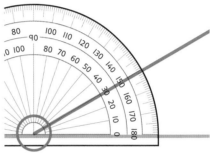

Step 3

Follow the scale from the zero mark to the completed turn. Read the angle from the scale.

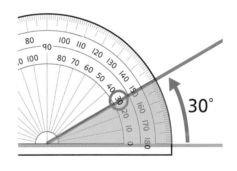

30°

The ramp is now at an angle of 30°.

b) Protractors often have two scales, so you can start measuring from the left or from the right. Amal's mistake is reading the wrong scale.

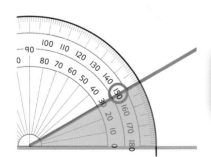

I can see that the angle is acute, because it is less than 90°. So I know which scale to read.

Think together

1 Between which angles could the trainer have slipped down the ramp?

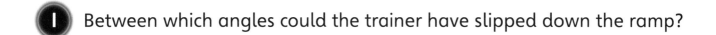

The trainer could have slipped down the ramp between ◻° and ◻°.

2 Measure these angles using a protractor.

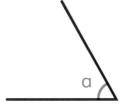

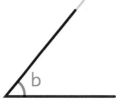

a

b

c

a = ◻°   b = ◻°   c = ◻°

I wonder if it helps to turn the page around?

3 Measure each of the angles in the triangles.

What do you notice?

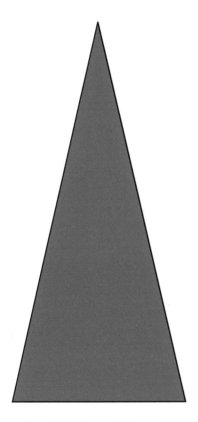

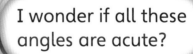

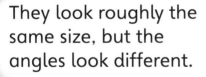
They look roughly the same size, but the angles look different.

I wonder if all these angles are acute?

79

→ **Practice book 5C p57**

Measuring with a protractor ❷

Discover

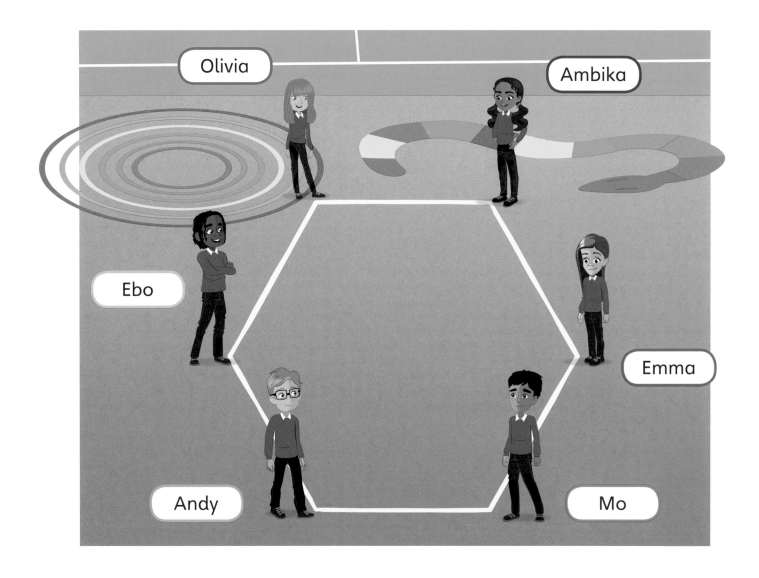

I **a)** Mo turns from facing Andy to face Emma. What angle does he turn?

b) Emma turns from facing Mo to face Ambika. What angle does she turn?

Share

a) This turn makes an obtuse angle. It is greater than 90°.

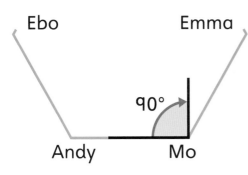

I know which scale to use on the protractor because the angle is greater than 90°, so it is obtuse.

Mo turns an angle of 120°.

b) Emma turns an angle of 120°.

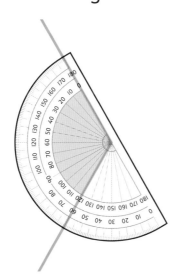

I noticed that each angle inside the hexagon is 120°.

Think together

1 Measure the angles shown with a protractor.

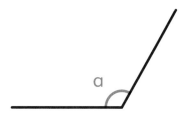

a is ⬚°.

b is ⬚°.

2 Put these angles in order, from smallest to greatest.

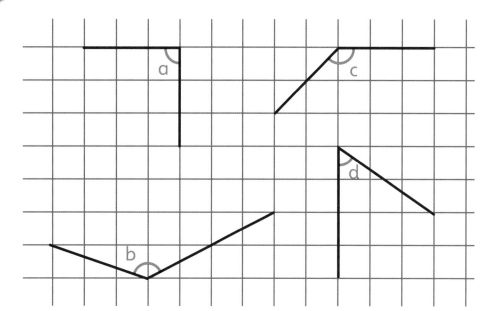

Smallest   Greatest

⬚ ⬚ ⬚ ⬚

I can work out which is the smallest angle without measuring.

3 **a)** Amelia stands in the centre facing A. She turns to face C.

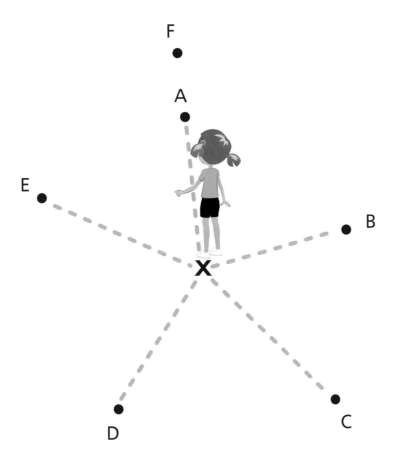

What angle does she turn?

I wonder if I could give two answers.

b) Then Amelia turns from facing C to face F.

What angle does she turn? What do you notice?

Drawing lines and angles accurately

Discover

It says not to scale, so I cannot just trace it.

Follow the steps

Step 1

75 mm

60°

60 mm

Step 2

60°

75 mm

Not to scale

1 **a)** These are the first two steps for a design.

Copy step 1 of the design accurately.

b) Copy step 2 of the design accurately.

Share

a) You need a ruler, a sharp pencil and a protractor.

Draw the horizontal 60 mm line first.

60 mm is the same as 6 cm.

Now place the protractor so that the centre is lined up with the turn.

Find 60° and mark a dot.

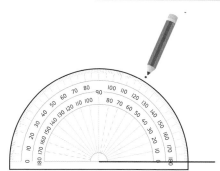

Line up your ruler with the corner and the dot, and draw a line of precisely 75 mm at 60°.

75 mm is the same as 7·5 cm.

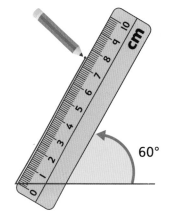

b) You will need to find the correct way to place your protractor.

Find 60° and mark a dot then draw a line of precisely 75 mm at 60°.

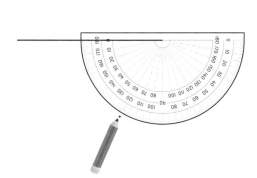

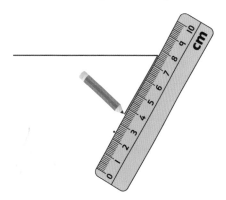

Think together

1 Copy step 3 of the design.

Step 3

75 mm

60° 60 mm

60°

75 mm 100 mm

10°

2 Copy step 4 of the design.

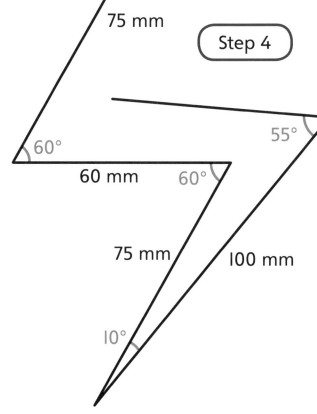

Step 4

75 mm

60°

60 mm 60°

55°

75 mm 100 mm

10°

3 **a)** Copy step 5 of the design.

CHALLENGE

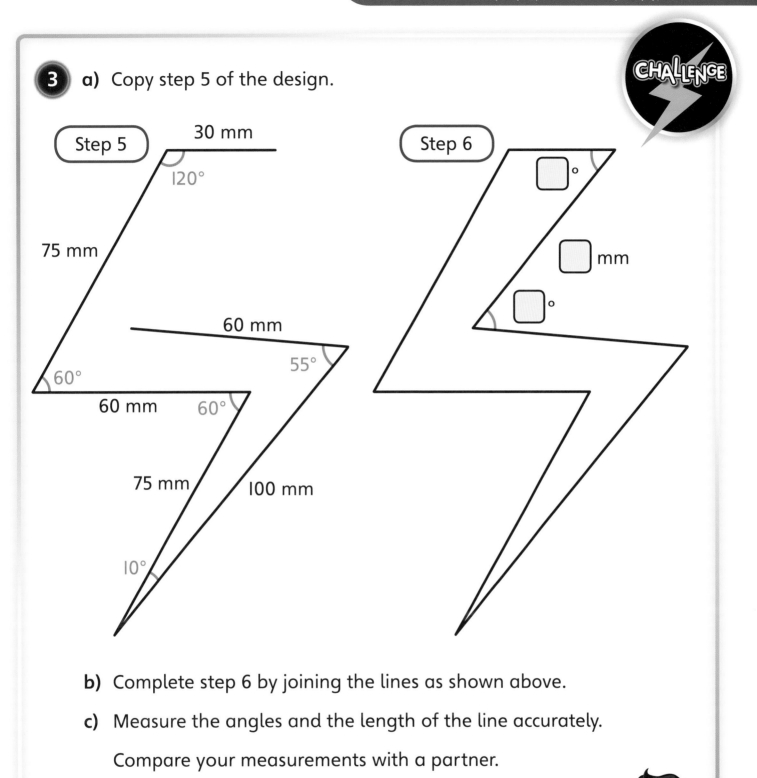

b) Complete step 6 by joining the lines as shown above.

c) Measure the angles and the length of the line accurately.

Compare your measurements with a partner.

I wonder why some measurements are different.

→ Practice book 5C p63

Calculating angles on a straight line

Discover

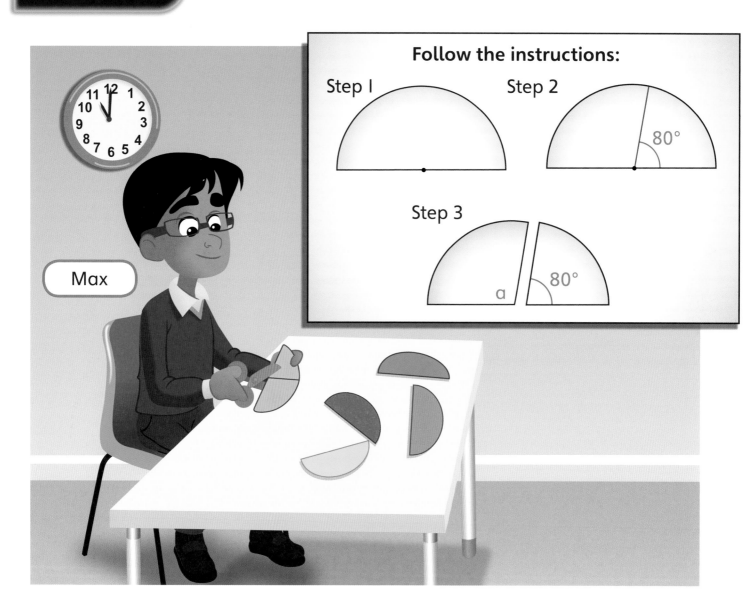

Max

Follow the instructions:

Step 1

Step 2
80°

Step 3
a   80°

1 **a)** What is the size of angle a?

b) Max copies the instructions on the whiteboard but does not measure accurately.

He cuts two equal angles instead.

What angle does he cut?

Share

a)

I measured angle a with a protractor.

It is 100°.

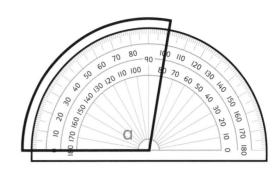

I calculated the missing angle. I know there are 180 degrees in a half-turn, so I worked out

180 – 80 = 100.

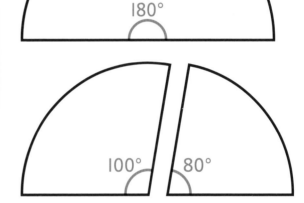

180°

100°   80°

The two angles would make a half turn, so the complete angle is 180°.

180 – 80 = 100

Angle a is 100°.

b) Half of 180 is 90. The two angles must be right angles, or quarter turns.

Max cuts two 90-degree angles.

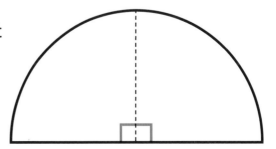

89

Think together

1. Predict the size of the missing angles. Then measure to check.

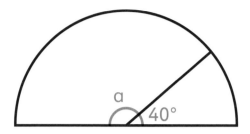

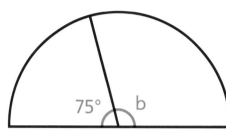

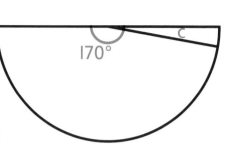

170°

a = ⬜ °

b = ⬜ °

c = ⬜ °

2. Which angles could fit together to make a straight line?

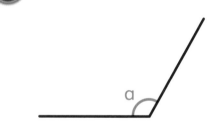

a

c

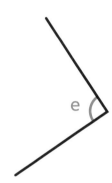

e

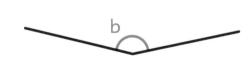

b

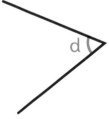

d

f

a = ⬜ °   b = ⬜ °   c = ⬜ °   d = ⬜ °   e = ⬜ °   f = ⬜ °

⬜ and ⬜ fit together to make a straight line.

⬜ and ⬜ fit together to make a straight line.

3 Max wants to split his angle into five equal parts. What is the size of each of the angles?

$a = \boxed{}°$

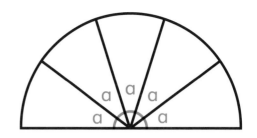

4 Isla rests a square on point P, which is on a straight line.

She measures the angle on either side as she rotates the square.

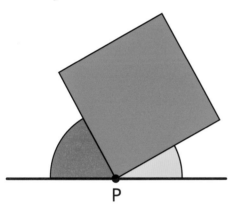

P

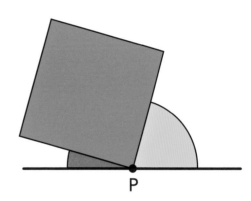

P

a) How can she make the left-hand angle and the right-hand angle equal?

b) Isla makes it so the left-hand angle is twice the size of the right-hand angle.

What is the size of each angle?

All three angles must total 180°. I already know the angle of the square.

91

Calculating angles around a point

Discover

How to make an angle-maker

Step 1: Cut a line to the centre of each circle.

Step 2: Slide the two circles together.

Step 3: Rotate the circles to show different angles.

1 **a)** How can the angle-maker be used to show a 90° angle?

b) When the angle-maker shows a 90° angle, what is the other angle it shows?

Share

a) A whole turn is 360°. A 90-degree angle is a quarter turn.

The angle-maker can be used in any of these ways to show a 90° angle.

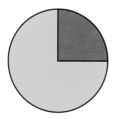 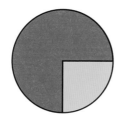 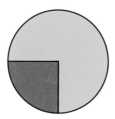 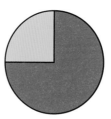

b) One right angle is a quarter turn, so there must be three quarter turns remaining.

90 + 90 + 90 = 270

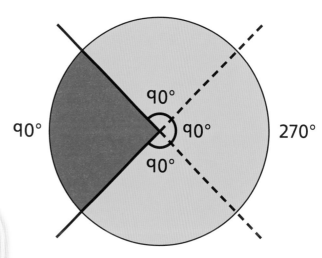

270° is a $\frac{3}{4}$ turn.

> I also know that a whole turn is 360°. I will subtract 90 from the whole turn.

360 – 90 = 270.

The other angle the angle-maker shows is 270°.

> I can use these circles to investigate other pairs of angles.

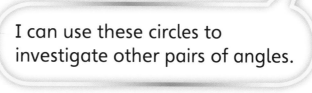

Think together

1 What angles are shown on this angle-maker?

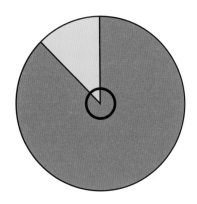

I will measure one angle, then calculate the other angle.

The angles are ☐° and ☐°.

2 Find the missing angles.

a)

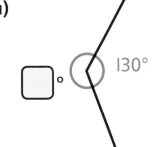

☐° 130°

c)

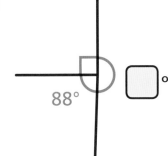

88° ☐°

b)

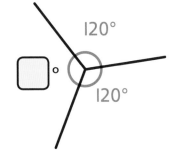

120°

☐° 120°

3 Jamilla wants to copy this angle.

My protractor only measures to 180°.

Jamilla

Angles bigger than 180° are called **reflex angles**.

I think Jamilla can use what we have learnt about angles today to draw this angle.

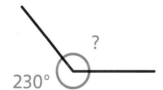

a) Explain how Jamilla could use her protractor to draw an angle of 230°.

b) Use this method to draw your own reflex angle of 230°.

Now draw an angle of 312°.

→ Practice book 5C p69

Calculating lengths and angles in shapes

Discover

1 a) What are the **interior angles** of the parallelogram?

b) Lee thinks length A must be 20 cm and length B must be 10 cm. Is he correct?

Share

a) The four angles in a square are all 90°.

This allows us to calculate the angles of the triangles.

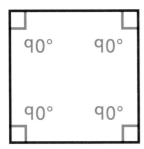 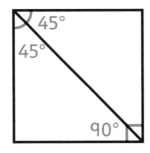

$90° \div 2 = 45°$

Now we can use this information to calculate the angles inside the parallelogram. We can call these interior angles.

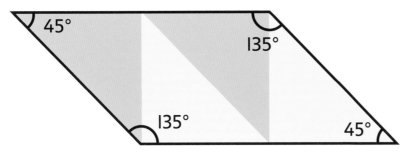

$90 + 45 = 135$

The interior angles of the parallelogram are: 45°, 45°, 135° and 135°.

b) Length A is two 10 cm lengths, so it must be 20 cm long.

Length B is the diagonal of one square. If you measure the length it is greater than 10 cm.

Lee is correct about length A, but wrong about length B.

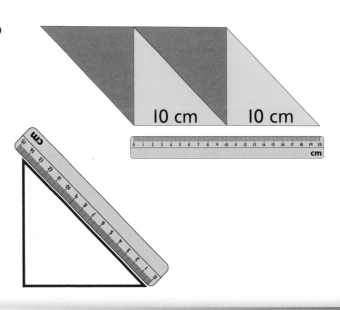

97

Think together

1 Lee fits together the four triangles in different ways. What angles can you work out without measuring?

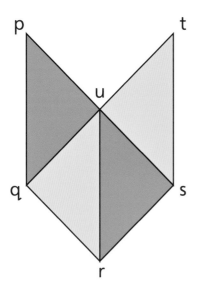
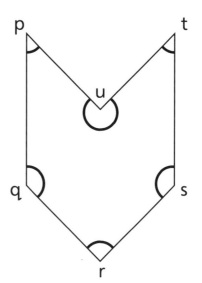

2 Work out the length and the width of Shape B.

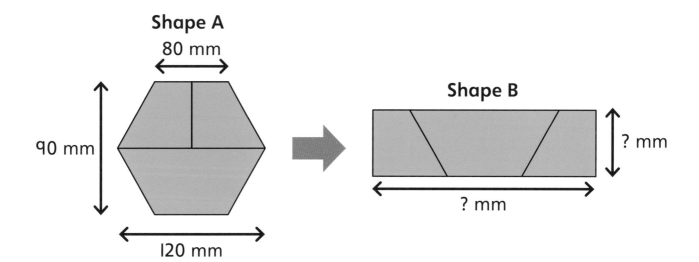

Shape A

80 mm

90 mm

120 mm

Shape B

? mm

? mm

Length = ☐ mm

Width = ☐ mm

3 Max splits a rectangle in half diagonally.

Each angle will be 45° because the rectangles are split exactly in half.

Max

Investigate this statement by checking what happens to the angles when you split these shapes in half. Is Max correct?

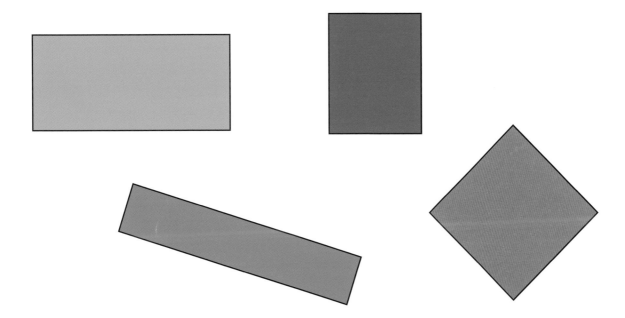

I will use trial and error and write my findings in a table.

→ Practice book 5C p72

End of unit check

1 Which shows a 180-degree turn?

A 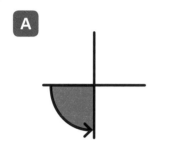 B 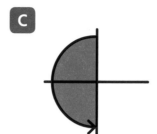 C 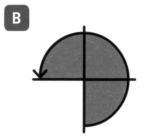 D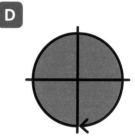

2 What angle does this show?

A 60°   B 45°   C 120°   D 30°

3 Explain the mistake.

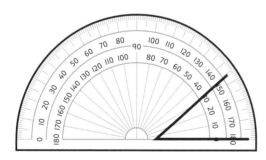

A The protractor is upside down.

B The centre is not lined up with the turn.

C The angle is obtuse so the protractor is not big enough.

D The base line is not lined up with one line of the angle.

100

4 Which missing angle is not 50°?

A

C
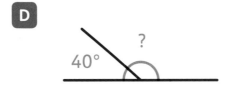

B
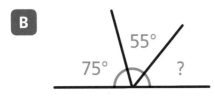

D
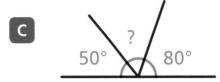

5 Each angle is equal. What is the angle?

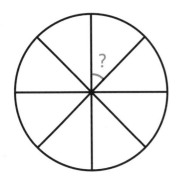

A 45°   B 30°   C 90°   D 360°

6 What is the angle labelled y? Explain your reasons.

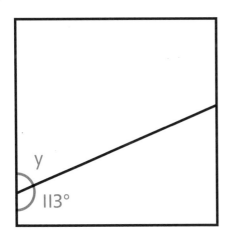

101

→ Practice book 5C p75

Unit 14
Geometry – properties of shapes ②

In this unit we will …

⚡ Recognise and draw parallel lines

⚡ Recognise and draw perpendicular lines

⚡ Label parallel and perpendicular lines with the correct notation

⚡ Accurately identify regular and irregular polygons

⚡ Recognise different 3D shapes from different views

Do you remember how to spot parallel lines? Can you see the pair that are not parallel?

We will need some maths words. Which one can mean an angle inside a 2D shape?

parallel   perpendicular   angle

right angle   interior angle   quadrilateral

view   regular   irregular

3D shape   pyramid   sphere   cone

hexagon   pentagon   triangle

top view   plan view   side view

We need to recognise shapes too. Can you find the one that is not a quadrilateral?

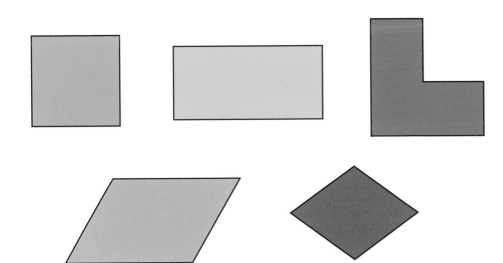

Recognising and drawing parallel lines

Discover

1 **a)** Which lines on the gates are parallel?

b) Explain why the diagonal lines on the gates are not parallel.

Share

a) All the horizontal and all the vertical lines on the gates are parallel.

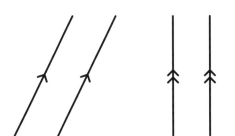

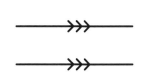

We can show parallel lines with arrow markings.

We can mark the parallel lines on the gates with arrows.

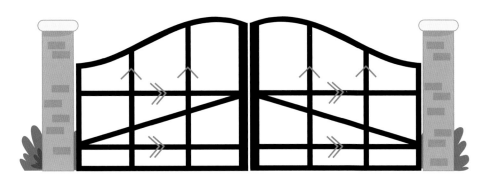

I wonder why there are different numbers of arrows on the horizontal and vertical lines.

b) The diagonal lines on the gates are not parallel because if they continued they would cross over.

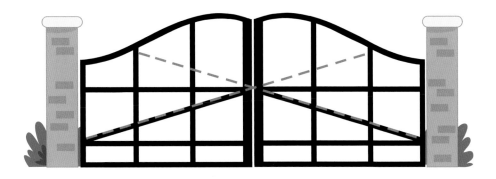

Think together

1 One of the gates has rusted from its hinges.

How many sets of parallel lines are there now?

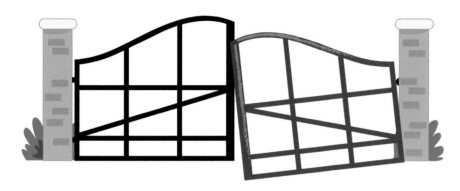

There are now ☐ sets of parallel lines.

2 Which sides should have arrow markings on to show that they are parallel?

a)

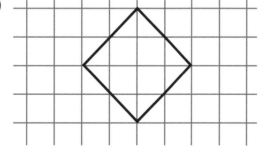

c)

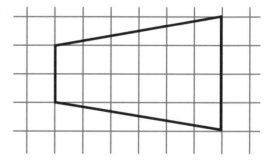

b)

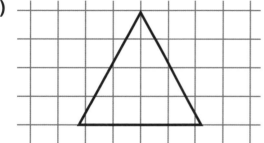

d)

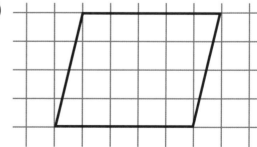

I wonder if parallel lines must be exactly the same length.

3 Max has drawn a shape and labelled every vertex.

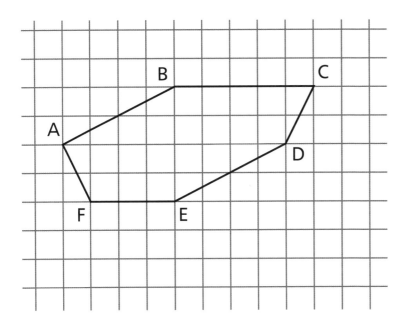

Line BC is parallel to line EF.

Max

a) Point to the lines Max is describing.

b) Which other lines are parallel? How do you know?

c) How would you draw lines parallel to AB or to BC on the grid below?

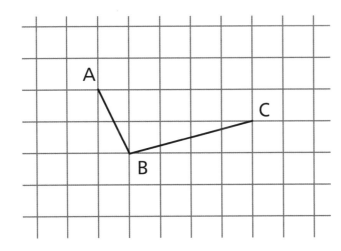

I will use the grid pattern to help me.

→ Practice book 5C p78

Recognising and drawing perpendicular lines

Discover

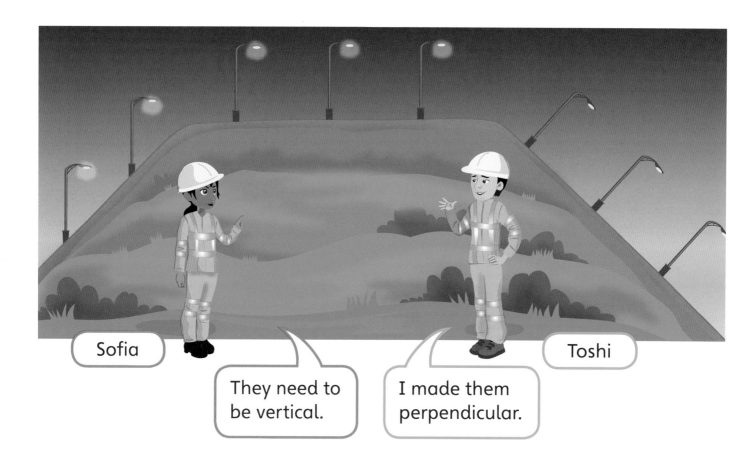

Sofia

They need to be vertical.

I made them perpendicular.

Toshi

1 **a)** Which streetlamps are perpendicular to the road?

b) Which streetlamps are both vertical and perpendicular?

Can you prove they are perpendicular?

Share

a) Perpendicular lines cross or meet at a 90-degree angle.

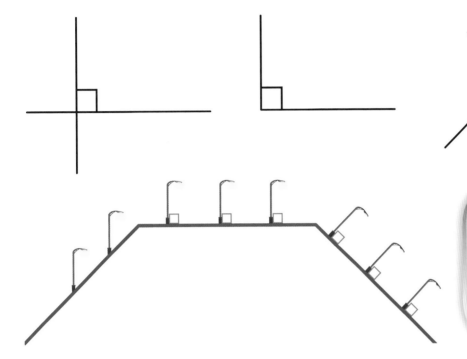

Remember, a 90-degree angle is also called a right angle. We show it with a box marking.

The streetlamps on the top of the hill and on the right are perpendicular to the road because they make right angles.

b) The road on top of the hill is horizontal, which is perpendicular to vertical.

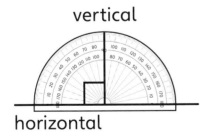

vertical

horizontal

The streetlamps on the top of the hill are both vertical and perpendicular to the road, making right angles.

I can prove this with a protractor.

Think together

1 Which of these diagrams show perpendicular lines?

A

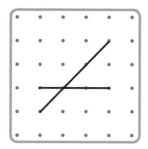

C

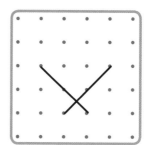

B

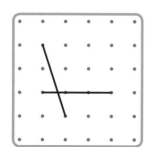

D

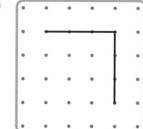

_____ show perpendicular lines.

2 **a)** Name the lines that are perpendicular to the line AB.

_____ are perpendicular to AB.

b) Point to the lines that are perpendicular to the line HI.

_____ are perpendicular to HI.

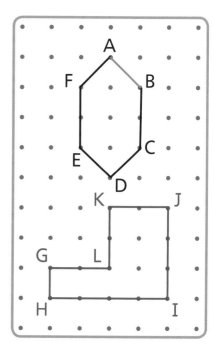

Perpendicular lines do not always have to touch or cross.

3 **a)** Bella thinks she has made rectangles on her geoboards.
Is she correct? Explain your answer.

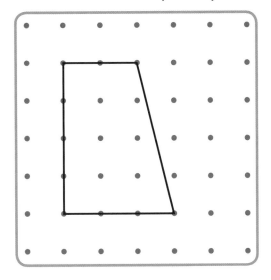 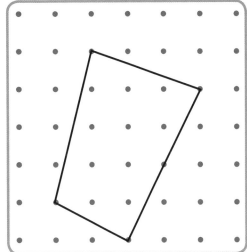

b) Explain how to complete the rectangles.

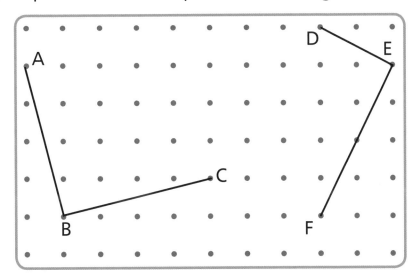

I wonder how I can make perpendicular lines to complete the rectangles.

I will look at the grid to help me make the perpendicular lines accurate.

III

Reasoning about parallel and perpendicular lines

Discover

1 **a)** Measure the angle where the plain red strip of paper crosses a dotted strip.

Is it the same each time?

b) How can you move the plain red strip of paper so that it is parallel to the stripy blue strip of paper?

Does it help to notice if there are any perpendicular lines?

Share

a) Use a protractor to measure the angle where the plain red strip of paper crosses each dotted strip of paper.

I measured the other side of the line and each angle was 30°.

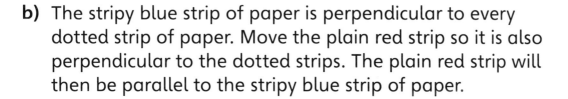

All the dotted strips of paper are parallel. The plain red strip crosses each dotted strip of paper at an angle of 150°. The angle is the same each time.

b) The stripy blue strip of paper is perpendicular to every dotted strip of paper. Move the plain red strip so it is also perpendicular to the dotted strips. The plain red strip will then be parallel to the stripy blue strip of paper.

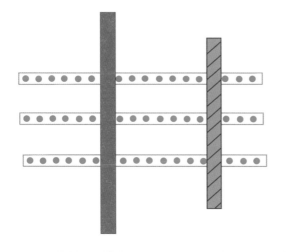

I will use a protractor to check the angle of the stripy blue strip.

113

Think together

1 How could you place a strip of paper parallel to the plain red strip?

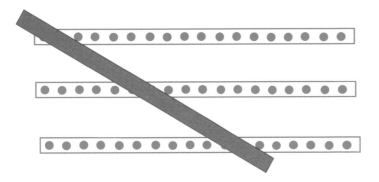

2 Isla folds a piece of paper. Identify any parallel and perpendicular lines.

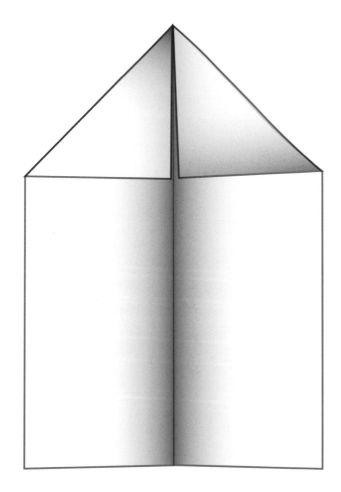

3 Max draws lines to join opposite corners of these shapes.

a) Which shapes have diagonals that are perpendicular?

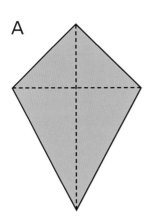

A

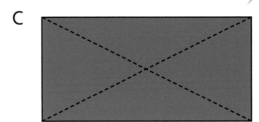

C

B

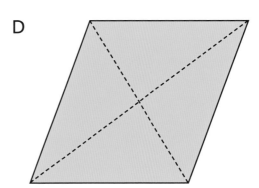

D

I think the diagonals of squares are always perpendicular.

b) Do you agree with Astrid? Explain your answer.

115

→ **Practice book 5C p84**

Regular and irregular polygons

Discover

1 a) Is Isla correct? How do you know?

b) Is Richard correct? How do you know?

Share

a) There are different methods to check the size of the angles.

I measured them with a protractor. They all measured the same.

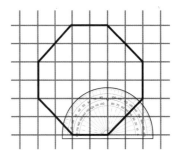

Each angle is made of a right angle and half a right angle. You can see this on the grid.

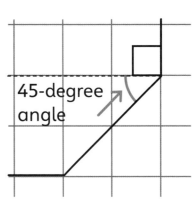

45-degree angle

$45° + 90° = 135°$

Every interior angle is 135°. Isla is correct.

b)

Regular shapes have:

All angles equal.

All sides the same length.

I know that if the angles are not all the same, or the sides are not all the same, then the shape is irregular.

The sides are not all the same length.

Richard is not correct. This is an irregular octagon.

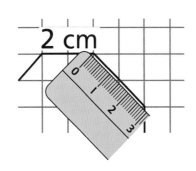

2 cm

117

Think together

1 Explain why each shape is irregular.

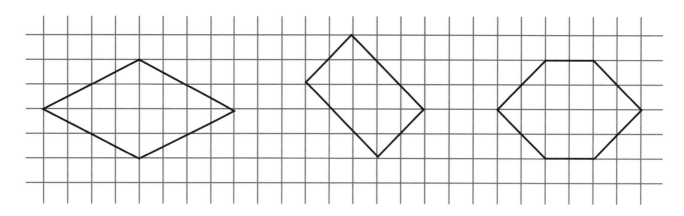

The rhombus is irregular because the _____ are not all the same size.

The rectangle is irregular because _____ .

The hexagon is _____ .

2 Measure the angles and the sides of the pentagons. Which one is regular? How do you know?

A   B   C

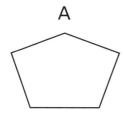 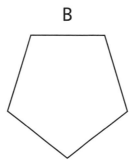 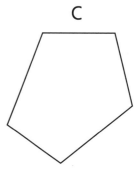

_____ is regular because _____ .

3 Max and Ambika are making shapes on different geoboards.

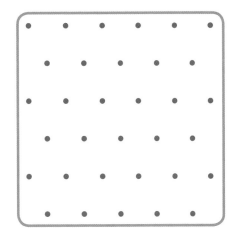

I will make a regular quadrilateral.

I will make a regular hexagon.

Max

Ambika

a) Which geoboard should each child use?

b) Which regular shapes could Max and Ambika make on the different boards?

c) Which regular shapes cannot be made on either board?

I will make a list of all the regular shapes I know and try to make them on a geoboard.

119

→ Practice book 5C p87

Reasoning about 3D shapes

Discover

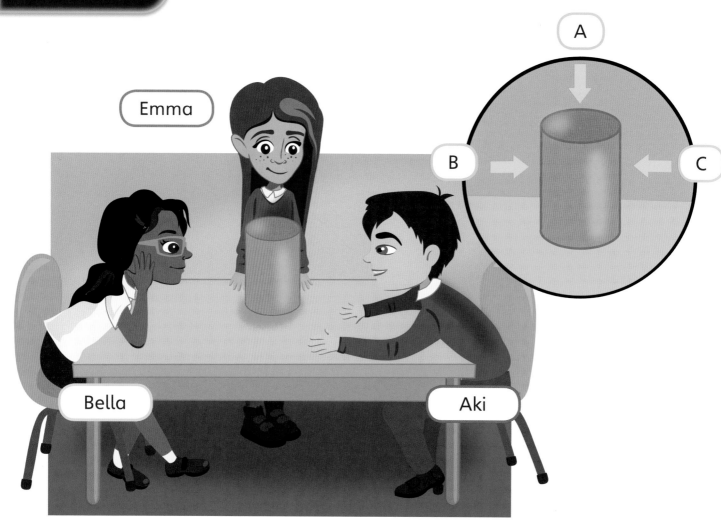

1 a) Emma looks at the shape from position A. What can she see?

b) Bella looks at the shape from position B and Aki looks at the shape from position C. What do they each see?

Share

a) Position A is a **top view**. Emma can see one face from this view.

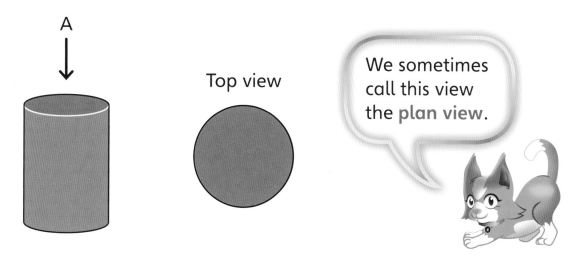

We sometimes call this view the **plan view**.

From position A, Emma can see only one face of the cylinder. The face is a circle.

b) Bella and Aki both have a **side view**. For this cylinder, each side view is a rectangle.

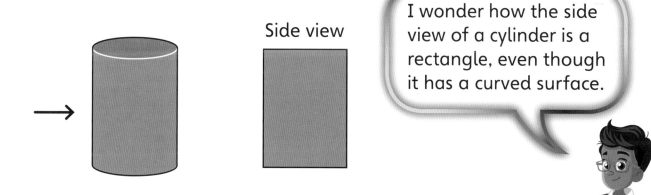

I wonder how the side view of a cylinder is a rectangle, even though it has a curved surface.

Bella and Aki each have the same side view of the cylinder. They each see a rectangle.

Think together

1 Which of the shapes A, B and C could not be a view of this cube? Explain to your partner why.

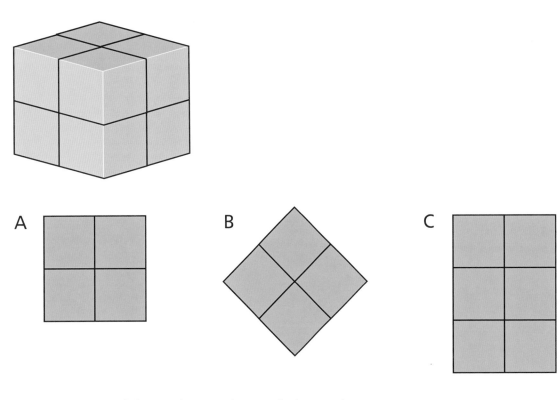

A

B

C

_____ could not be a view of the cube.

2 Luis, Andy and Jamie look at this prism from different positions. Describe and draw what they can each see.

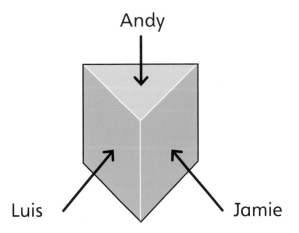

Andy

Luis

Jamie

3 Max looks at this collection of 3D shapes from above.

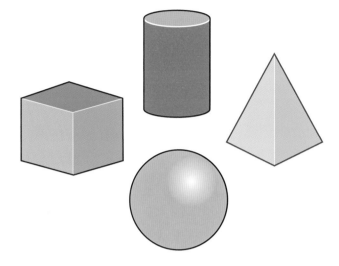

Which of these could be what he sees?

A

C

B

D

I will think carefully about which shapes are next to each other.

→ Practice book 5C p90

End of unit check

1 Which shape does not have any parallel lines?

A

B

C

D

2 Which diagram shows perpendicular lines?

A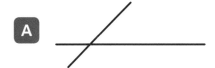

B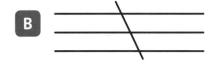

C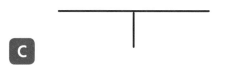

D

3 Which shape has one pair of parallel lines and no perpendicular lines?

A

B

C

D

4 Which set has one irregular and one regular shape?

A

C

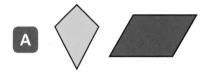

B

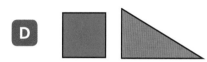

D

5 Which shape does not have a view that is a rectangle?

A

C

B

D

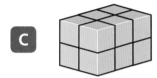

6 Sketch the top and side views of this shape.

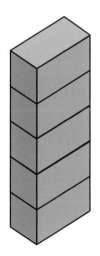

→ Practice book 5C p93

Unit 15
Geometry – position and direction

In this unit we will ...

⚡ Learn to reflect simple 2D shapes in vertical and horizontal lines

⚡ Plot and find coordinates of a reflected point on a grid

⚡ Use coordinates to calculate new points of a reflected shape

⚡ Translate 2D shapes on grid paper

⚡ Use coordinates to find translations

We will be reflecting shapes in a mirror line and using coordinates. What are the coordinates of this reflected shape? Do you notice anything about the reflection?

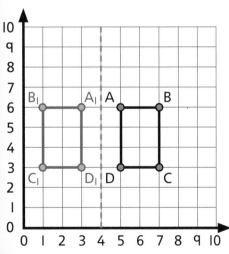

Here are some maths words we will be using. Are any of these words new?

reflection   translation   vertex

vertices   coordinates   mirror line

horizontal axis   vertical axis

We need to be able to work out the distance between coordinates on a grid. How far apart are the coordinates A and B?

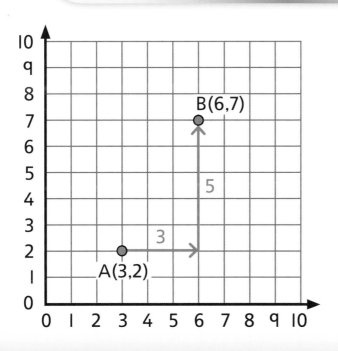

Reflection

Discover

What will this triangle look like in a mirror? Reflect the shape by placing a mirror on each line.

Mrs Dean

Olivia

I **a)** What will the reflection be when the mirror is placed on line L₁?

b) Draw the reflection when the mirror is placed on line L₃.

Share

a) Each vertex must be the same distance from the **mirror line**.

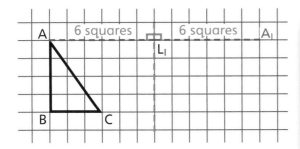

Vertex A is six squares from the mirror line, so I need to count six squares the other side of the line.

Vertex C is three squares from the line, so the new vertex C_1 must be three squares from the mirror line too.

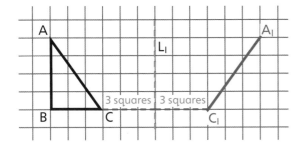

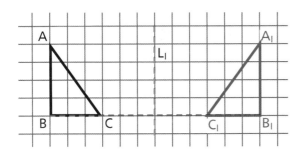

I can see where vertex B_1 should go because it is below vertex A_1 and level with vertex C_1.

b)

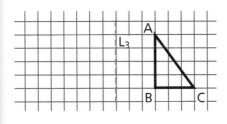
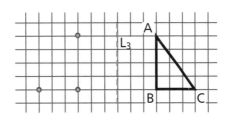
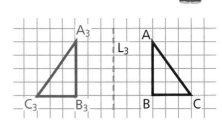

129

Think together

1 Complete the reflection of the triangle in L₂.

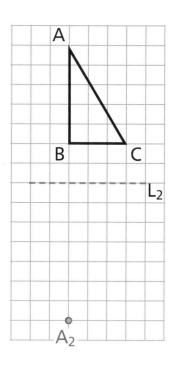

2 Bella drew the symmetric figure of ABC, reflected in the mirror line L₄.

Explain her mistake. Then draw the correct reflection on squared paper.

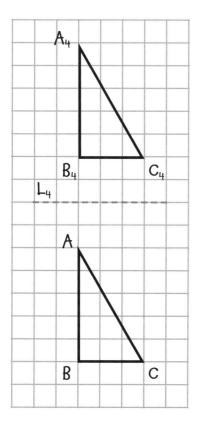

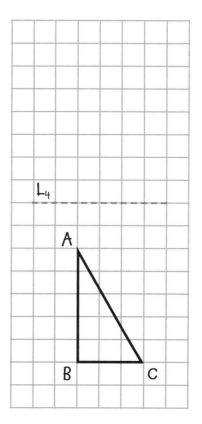

3 **a)** Max has used reflection to turn 'M' into 'W'.

Explain how to use reflection to turn 'q' into '6'.

> I wonder if you might have to reflect the shape more than once.

> I will try more than one way to turn q into 6.

b) Predict what the letter V will look like when it is reflected in the dotted line. Then use the isometric grid to trace the reflection of the letter V.

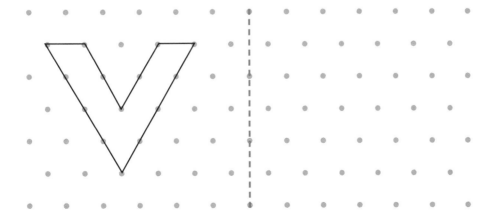

131

→ **Practice book 5C p96**

Reflection with coordinates

Discover

T marks the spot, but the real location of the treasure is the reflection of point T in the line L.

Jen

Toshi

1 a) Reflect the point T in the mirror line. What are the true coordinates of the treasure?

b) There is a secret cave at the reflection of coordinates (6,8). What are the coordinates of the secret cave?

Share

a) T is at the coordinates (2,3).

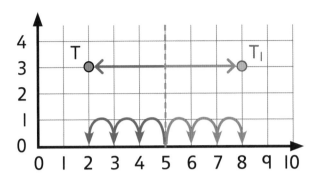

Remember, we always put the number across first, so (2,3) means 2 along and 3 up.

The new horizontal coordinate must be 5 + 3 = 8.

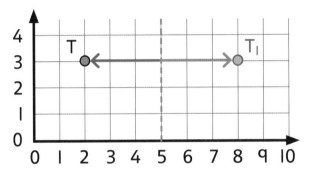

I will count how many squares T is from the mirror line. The reflected point must be the same distance away on the other side.

The true coordinates of the treasure, T₁, are (8,3).

I notice that the second part of the coordinates does not change.

b) The first part of the coordinates is 1 away from the mirror line to the right: 5 + 1 = 6

The reflected coordinate is also 1 away, to the left: 5 − 1 = 4

The second part of the coordinates stays the same (**8**).

The coordinates of the secret cave are (4,8).

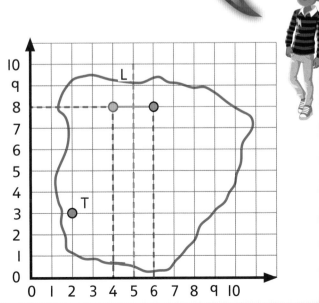

Think together

1 Max marks three points with counters. Aki reflects the points in the mirror line and places a counter on each of the reflected points.

What are the coordinates of each reflected point?

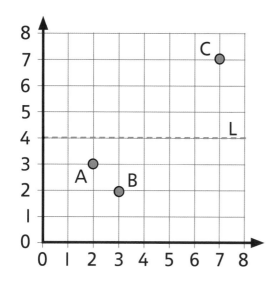

Max's counters are placed at:
A(2,3)
B(3,2)
C(7,7)

Aki's counters will be placed at:

A₁(☐ , ☐)

B₁(☐ , ☐)

C₁(☐ , ☐)

2 The rectangle on this grid is reflected in the line L₁.

Write the coordinates of the reflected rectangle.

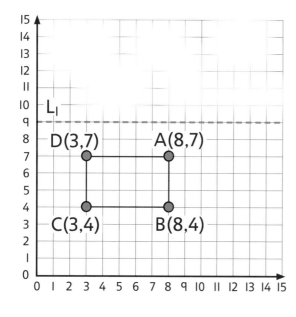

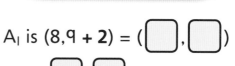

I wonder which part of the coordinates will not change.

A₁ is (8, 9 + 2) = (☐ , ☐)

B₁ is (☐ , ☐)

C₁ is (☐ , ☐)

D₁ is (☐ , ☐)

3 **a)** The rectangle is reflected in the mirror line. What are the coordinates of the reflected vertices?

CHALLENGE

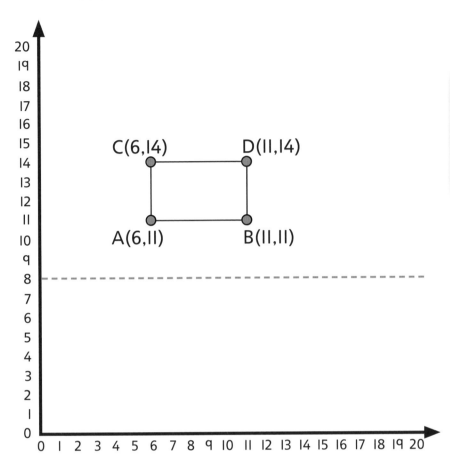

C(6,14)   D(11,14)

A(6,11)   B(11,11)

I cannot see the grid lines so I will use the coordinates to calculate the new position.

A₁ is (⬚ , ⬚)

B₁ is (⬚ , ⬚)

C₁ is (⬚ , ⬚)

D₁ is (⬚ , ⬚)

b) Write the coordinates of the triangle and of the reflected triangle.

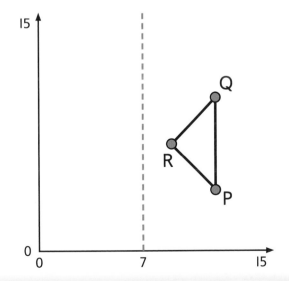

P = (⬚ , ⬚)   P₁ = (⬚ , ⬚)

Q = (⬚ , ⬚)   Q₁ = (⬚ , ⬚)

R = (⬚ , ⬚)   R₁ = (⬚ , ⬚)

135

Translation

Discover

I will slide the bed 5 squares to the left.

Bella

bed

table

desk

wardrobe

1 **a)** What will be the new position of Bella's bed?

b) Bella decides to move the table. She slides it 8 squares to the right, then 6 squares down. Where will the table be now?

Share

a) When a shape slides across a grid, this is called a **translation**.

> I know that each vertex moves 5 squares to the left.

Point A moves 5 squares to the left.

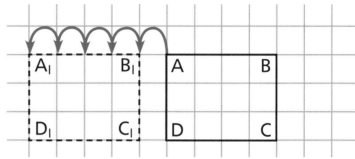

Each vertex moves 5 squares to the left.

> A common mistake is to think that there must be a gap of 5 between the old position and the new position.

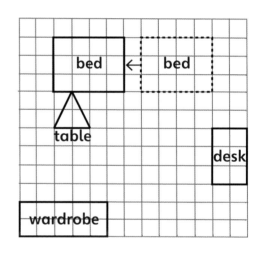

The new position of Bella's bed will be above the table.

b) Bella moves the table 8 squares to the right. Then she moves it 6 squares down.

> A translation moves left or right first, then up or down. This is like coordinates.

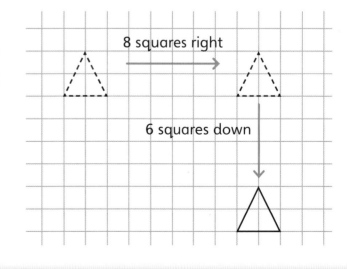

The table will now be in the bottom right corner of her room, near the desk.

137

Think together

① This desk is translated to a new position, shown by the dotted lines. Describe the translation.

The desk has moved ☐ squares

_____ .

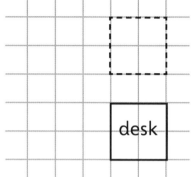

② a) Describe the translation from square A to square B, and from B to A.

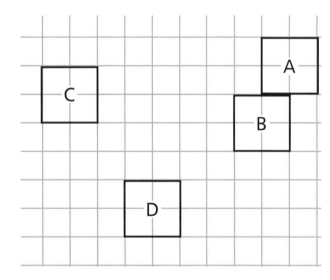

Your answer must show how many squares each vertex has moved left or right first, then up or down.

A to B: ☐ left and 2 _____

B to A: ☐ _____ and ☐ _____

b) Describe the translation from C to D and from D to C.

C to D: ☐ _____ and ☐ _____

D to C: ☐ _____ and ☐ _____

c) What do you notice?

138

3 **a)** The shaded triangle, A, is translated and reflected. Which triangles show reflections and which triangles show translations? How can you tell?

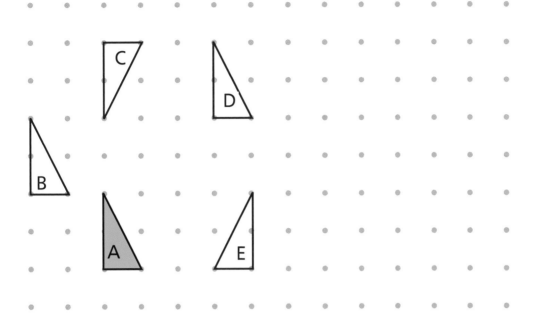

I can spot translations by imagining the shape sliding smoothly.

b) Describe each translation.

c) Where are the mirror lines for the reflections?

I can test for reflections by using a mirror.

d) Triangle A is translated 10 right and 3 up. Point to its new position on the grid.

139

→ Practice book 5C p102

Translation with coordinates

Discover

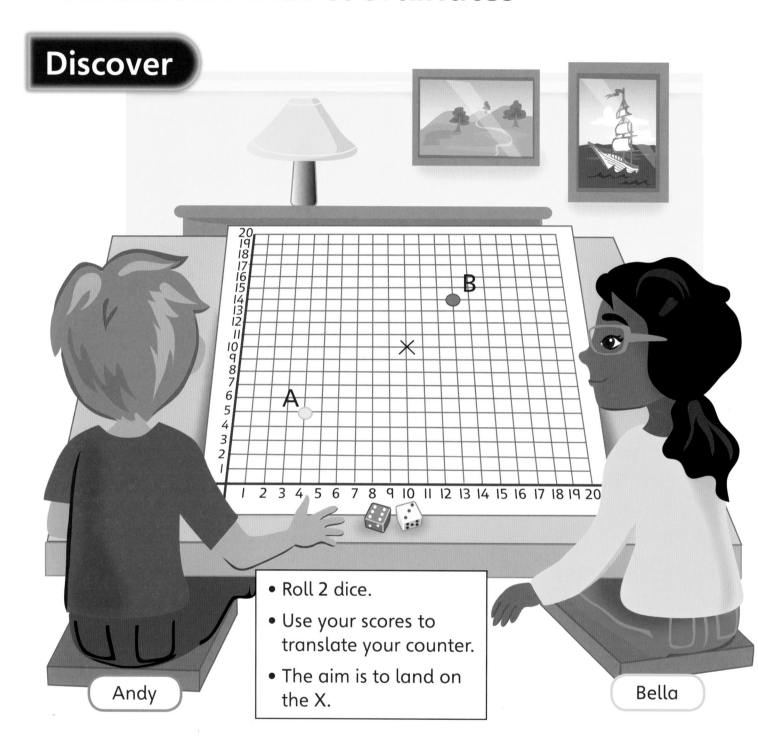

- Roll 2 dice.
- Use your scores to translate your counter.
- The aim is to land on the X.

Andy

Bella

1 a) Andy has the yellow counter (A). He chooses to translate 6 right and 3 up. What are the coordinates of his new position?

b) What translation would win for Bella's counter (B)?

Share

a) Andy's counter is at (4,5).

> I can count the grid squares to find the new position.

> I used the coordinates to calculate the new position. This is more efficient.

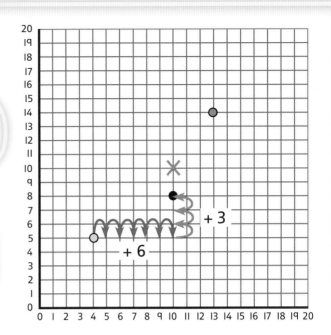

The starting position is (4,5).

A translation 6 right increases the horizontal coordinate by 6.

$4 + 6 = 10$

A translation 3 up increases the vertical coordinate by 3.

$5 + 3 = 8$

The coordinates of Andy's new position are (10,8).

b) Bella is on position (13,14). She wants to land on (10,10).

She needs to decrease the horizontal coordinate by 3. $13 - 3 = 10$. This is a translation 3 left.

She needs to decrease the vertical coordinate by 4. $14 - 4 = 10$. This is a translation 4 down.

A translation of 3 left, 4 down would win for Bella's counter.

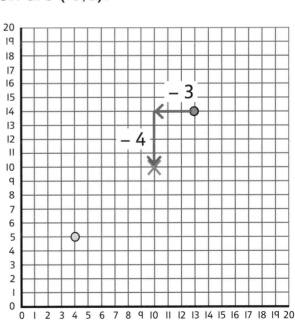

Think together

1 The boat is translated 6 right then 3 down. What are the coordinates of A and B after each translation?

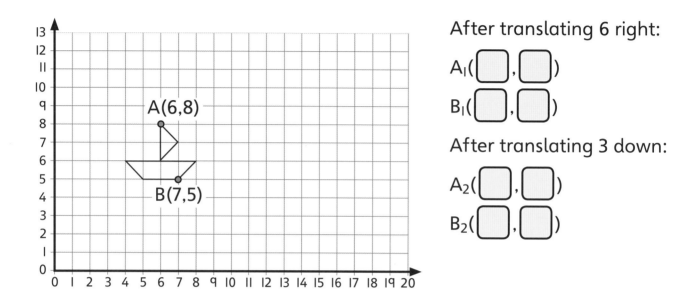

After translating 6 right:

A_1(☐,☐)

B_1(☐,☐)

After translating 3 down:

A_2(☐,☐)

B_2(☐,☐)

2 What are the coordinates of this square after a translation 10 right and 8 up?

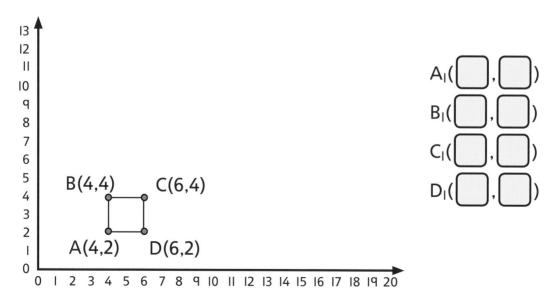

A_1(☐,☐)

B_1(☐,☐)

C_1(☐,☐)

D_1(☐,☐)

3 **a)** A triangle has been translated 11 left and 9 down.

What were the coordinates of the original triangle?

CHALLENGE

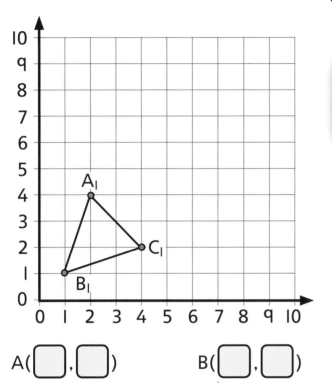

I will have to use the coordinates because the original triangle will go off the grid I have.

A(⬚ , ⬚)　　　B(⬚ , ⬚)　　　C(⬚ , ⬚)

b) A triangle has been translated 6 right and 6 up. What were the coordinates of its starting position?

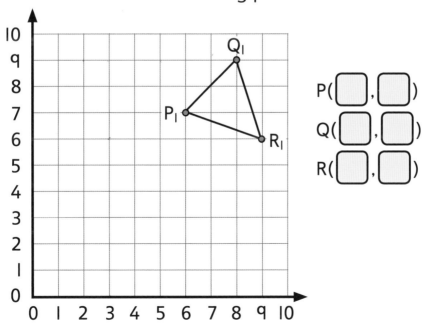

P(⬚ , ⬚)

Q(⬚ , ⬚)

R(⬚ , ⬚)

→ **Practice book 5C p105**

End of unit check

1 Which reflection is correct?

A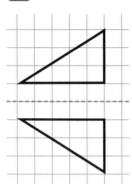

B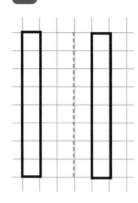

C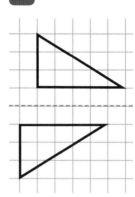

D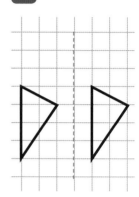

2 The point P is reflected in the mirror line. What are the coordinates of the reflected point?

A (3,5)

B (5,3)

C (9,8)

D (9,5)

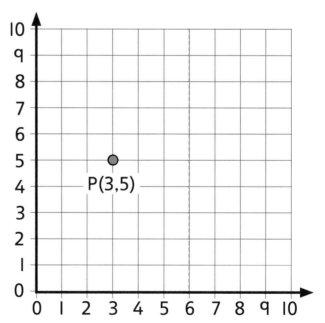

3 Which diagram shows shape A translated by 4 right and 3 up?

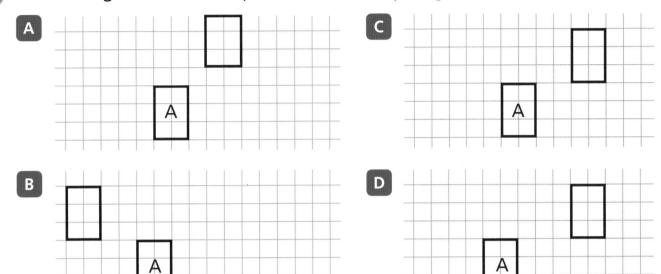

4 The isosceles triangle is reflected in the mirror line. What is the coordinate of the reflected point P?

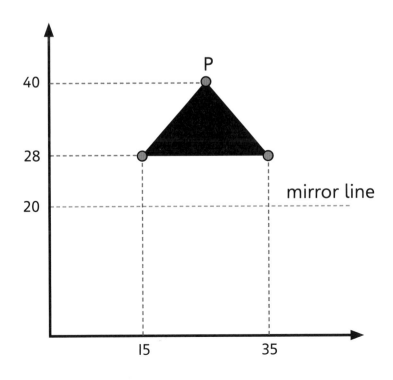

145

→ Practice book 5C p108

Unit 16
Measure – converting units

In this unit we will ...

⚡ Convert between metric units of length, mass and capacity

⚡ Recognise imperial units and understand how to convert them into metric units

⚡ Convert between units of time

⚡ Read timetables and understand the information they show

⚡ Solve problems based on measures

How many centimetres are approximately the same as 5 inches?

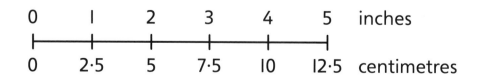

| 0 | 1 | 2 | 3 | 4 | 5 | inches |
| 0 | 2·5 | 5 | 7·5 | 10 | 12·5 | centimetres |

Here are some maths words we will be using. Are any of these words new?

convert   metric units   imperial units
kilo   kilogram   gram   millimetre
centimetre   metre   kilometre
litre   millilitre   pound (lb)   ounce (oz)
inch (in)   foot (ft)   yard (yd)
pint   gallon   stone (st)
approximately   timetable

How many millilitres of orange juice are in this jug?

Metric units ①

Discover

① **a)** How many metres is it from London to Berlin?

b) Can Jen take her bag on to the plane?

Share

a) Kilometres (km) and kilograms (kg) both begin with '**kilo**'.

1 km
1,000 m

The prefix 'kilo' comes from Greek. It means 'thousand'.

1 kilometre = 1,000 metres

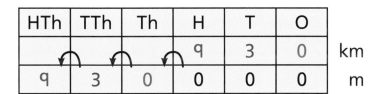

930 km

1 km	1 km	1 km		1 km
1,000 m	1,000 m	1,000 m		1,000 m

930 × 1,000

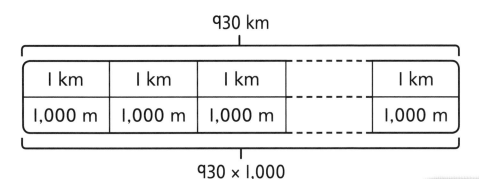

HTh	TTh	Th	H	T	O	
			9	3	0	km
9	3	0	0	0	0	m

To convert between kilometres and metres, I need to multiply by 1,000. I know that I can do this by moving each digit three places to the left.

9 hundreds become 9 hundred thousands.

3 tens become 3 ten thousands.

930 × 1,000 = 930,000

It is 930,000 metres from London to Berlin.

b) 1 kilogram = 1,000 grams

Th	H	T	O	•	Tth	Hth	
6	0	0	0	•			g
			6	•			kg

6,000 ÷ 1,000 = 6

6 kg < 7 kg, so Jen can take her bag onto the plane.

> I am converting from a smaller unit (grams) into a larger unit (kilograms), so I am going to divide this time.

Think together

1 These scales measure mass in grams.

What will the scales show when the rucksack is placed on them?

1 kg = ☐ g

To convert kg to g, multiply by ☐.

When we multiply by 1,000, the digits shift to the left by ☐ places.

Th	H	T	O	•	Tth	
			5	•	9	kg
5				•		g

5.9 × ☐ = ☐

The scales will show ☐ g when the rucksack is placed on them.

2 How many kilometres does this plane travel?

City A ·---------------- 260,500 m ----------→· City B

□ m = 1 km

To convert m to km, ◯ by □ .

The digits will shift to the _____ by □ places.

HTh	TTh	Th	H	T	O	•	Tth	Hth	Thth
2	6	0	5	0	0	•			

260,500 ◯ □ = □

The plane travels □ km.

---

3 Lee is working out how many grams are in 8·3 kilograms.

CHALLENGE

I know how to multiply by 1,000 quickly. I am going to write three zeros on the end.

Lee

It is not as easy as that! I think I need to shift the digits.

What mistake has Lee made?

How can you work out the correct answer?

→ Practice book 5C p111

Metric units ②

Discover

1 a) Has Ebo got enough fencing to go across the flower bed?

b) How many litres of water has Alex put in the watering can?

Share

The prefix 'milli' comes from Latin. We use it to mean 'one thousandth' of something.

a) Millimetres and millilitres both begin with '**milli**'.

1 m = 100 cm and 1 cm = 10 mm

100 × 10 = 1,000 so there are 1,000 millimetres in 1 metre.

1 millimetre = $\frac{1}{1,000}$ of a metre

Ebo has 1,500 mm of fencing. The flower bed is 2 m long.

2 × 1,000 = 2,000

2 ones are now worth 2 thousands.

1,500 < 2,000, so Ebo does not have enough fencing to go across the flower bed.

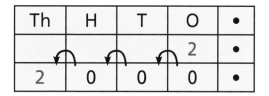

Th	H	T	O	•	
			2	•	m
2	0	0	0	•	mm

2 m

1 m	1 m
1,000 mm	1,000 mm

2,000 mm

b) Alex has 4,500 ml of water.

1,000 millilitres = 1 litre, so I am going to divide by 1,000 to convert from millilitres to litres.

4,500 ml

1,000 ml	1,000 ml	1,000 ml	1,000 ml	500 ml
1 l	1 l	1 l	1 l	0·5 l

4·5 l

4,500 ÷ 1,000 = 4·5

Alex has put 4·5 litres of water in the watering can.

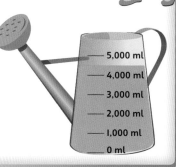

153

Think together

1 **a)** This flower is just starting to grow.

How tall is it in centimetres?

There are [ ] mm in 1 cm, so to convert mm into cm, divide by [ ] .

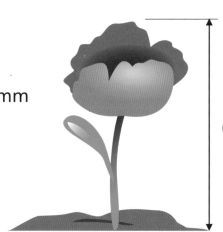

6 mm

O	•	Tth	
6	•		mm
0	•	6	cm

6 mm

1 mm	1 mm	1 mm	1 mm	1 mm	1 mm
0·1 cm	0·1 cm	0·1 cm	0·1 cm	0·1 cm	0·1 cm

[ ]

6 ÷ [ ] = [ ]

The flower is [ ] cm tall.

b) How many millilitres of plant food are in the bottle?

There are [ ] ml in 1 l.

H	T	O	•	Tth	
		0	•	7	l
			•		ml

PLANT FOOD

0·7 litres

0·7 ◯ [ ] = [ ]

The bottle contains [ ] ml.

2 Choose which operation goes into each sentence.

To convert from a larger to a smaller unit
(for example, from litres to ml), _____ .

To convert from a smaller to a larger unit
(for example, from mm to cm), _____ .

CHALLENGE

3 **a)** Complete the table.

Length	Capacity
1 mm = $\frac{1}{\Box}$ of a metre	1 ml = $\frac{1}{\Box}$ of a litre
1 cm = $\frac{1}{\Box}$ of a metre	
1 m = 1,000 _____	1 l = 1,000 _____
1 m = 100 _____	
1 _____ is 0·001 _____	1 _____ is 0·001 _____

Explain your answers.

b) What is the same about the two columns? What is different?

For the last line, I looked at the place value of the digit 1 to help me.

I can think of more than one possible answer for length in that part!

→ **Practice book 5C p114**

Metric units ❸

Discover

1 a) Is Isla tall enough to go on the roller coaster?

b) How many millilitres of fizzy pop is Aki buying altogether?

Share

a) Isla needs to convert 140 cm into metres.

140 cm ⟶ ? m

Smaller unit ⟶ larger unit, so we need to divide.

Divide by 100 as there are 100 cm in 1 m.

H	T	O	•	Tth	Hth
1	4	0	•		
		1	•	4	0

> The number line helps you convert between cm (along the top) and m (along the bottom).

140 ÷ 100 = 1·40   140 cm = 1·40 m = 1·4 m

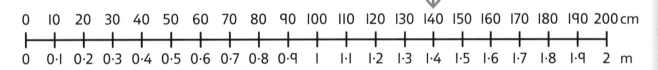

1·40 m < 1·45 m so Isla is not tall enough to go on the roller coaster.

b) Aki buys one 0·25 l bottle and one 500 ml bottle.

Larger unit ⟶ smaller unit, so we need to multiply.

> The question asks for the answer to be given in millilitres. One of the amounts is in litres, so I am going to convert it first.

Multiply by 1,000 as there are 1,000 ml in 1 l.

0·25 × 1,000 = 250, so 0·25 l = 250 ml

250 ml + 500 ml = 750 ml

Aki is buying 750 ml of fizzy pop altogether.

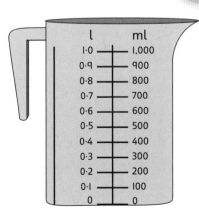

Think together

1 What should Ambika's total guess be?

The larger cake looks like it might weigh about 0·9 kg.

The smaller cake looks like it might weigh about 0·3 kg.

Ambika

Guess the total mass of the cakes!

Answers in grams please!

$0.9 \times 1,000 =$ ☐

H	T	O	•	Tth
		0	•	9
			•	

H	T	O	•	Tth
		0	•	3
			•	

$0.3 \times 1,000 =$ ☐

0.9 kg $=$ ☐ g 0.3 kg $=$ ☐ g

0.9 kg $+ 0.3$ kg $=$ ☐ g $+$ ☐ g $=$ ☐ g

Ambika should guess a total of ☐ g.

2 How long is the roller coaster now?

Give your answer in metres.

The roller coaster is now ☐ m long.

Please note: Due to a broken track, our 600 m roller coaster is now 300 cm shorter!

3 Here are the masses of five parcels.

A   B   C   D   E

a) Put the masses in order from heaviest to lightest.

I think you can just look at the position of the dial. The further around it is, the heavier it will be.

I am going to convert the masses of the parcels into the same unit.

b) If you converted the masses to a different unit, would you get the same order?

Explain your answer.

159

Metric units 4

Discover

1 a) How many 1p coins do the children need to lay flat to make a line 1 km long?

How much money will they have raised for charity?

b) How much more money would the children raise if they use Zac's idea and placed the coins on their sides?

Share

a) The base metric unit of length is the metre.

1 m
100 cm
1,000 mm

1 **milli**metre = $\frac{1}{1,000}$ m   1 **centi**metre = $\frac{1}{100}$ m

1 **kilo**metre = 1,000 m

1 1p coin is 1 cm long.

100 1p coins will be 1 metre long.

There are 1,000 m in 1 km.

$100 \times 1,000 = 100,000$

The children will need 100,000 1p coins to make a line 1 km long.

We know that 100p = £1.

$100,000 \div 100 = 1,000$

They will have raised £1,000 for charity.

> I did it a different way. I know there is 100p in £1 and that 100p is the same as 100 cm which is 1 m. So I multiplied £1 by 1,000 m to get £1,000.

b) 1 cm = 10 mm

So there are 10 coins for every 1 cm.

1 m = 100 cm

So in 1 m there are $10 \times 100 = 1,000$ coins.

1,000p = £10   1 km = 1,000 m

So, 1 km must be $£10 \times 1,000 = £10,000$

£10,000 − £1,000 = £9,000

The children would raise £9,000 more if they placed the coins on their sides.

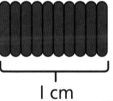

1 cm

1 m
100 cm

100 ×

1 cm

= 1,000p = £10

Think together

 Olivia makes a chain of coins 600 mm long. Each coin is I cm wide.

Use both methods to work out how many metres her chain of coins is.

Method I

I cm = 10 mm

To convert mm ⟶ cm, ÷ 10

▢ ÷ ▢ = ▢

600 mm = ▢ cm

H	T	O	
6	0	0	mm
			cm

To convert cm ⟶ m, ÷ 100

▢ ÷ ▢ = ▢

▢ cm = ▢ m

T	O	•	Tth	Hth	
		•			cm
		•			m

Olivia's chain of coins is ▢ m long.

Method 2

I m = 1,000 mm

To convert mm ⟶ m, ÷ 1,000

▢ ÷ ▢ = ▢

600 mm = ▢ m

H	T	O	•	Tth	Hth	THth	
6	0	0	•				mm
			•				m

Olivia's chain of coins is ▢ m long.

2 **a)** Max walks $\frac{1}{2}$ km to Bella's house.

Put these steps in the correct order to show how to work out how far he walks in centimetres.

> **A** Change m into cm by multiplying by 100.

> **B** Convert $\frac{1}{2}$ to a decimal.

> **C** Change km into m by multiplying by 1,000.

b) Now work out the answer.

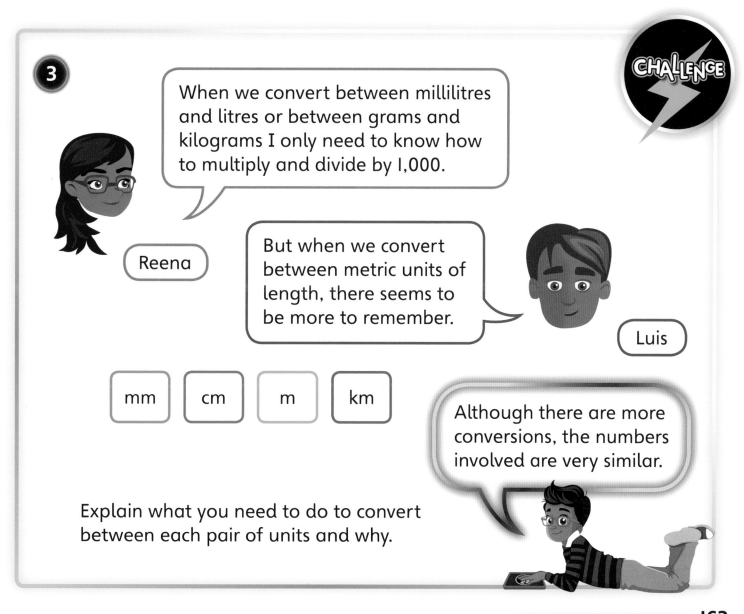

3

When we convert between millilitres and litres or between grams and kilograms I only need to know how to multiply and divide by 1,000.

Reena

But when we convert between metric units of length, there seems to be more to remember.

Luis

CHALLENGE

mm   cm   m   km

Although there are more conversions, the numbers involved are very similar.

Explain what you need to do to convert between each pair of units and why.

163

→ Practice book 5C p120

Imperial units of length

Discover

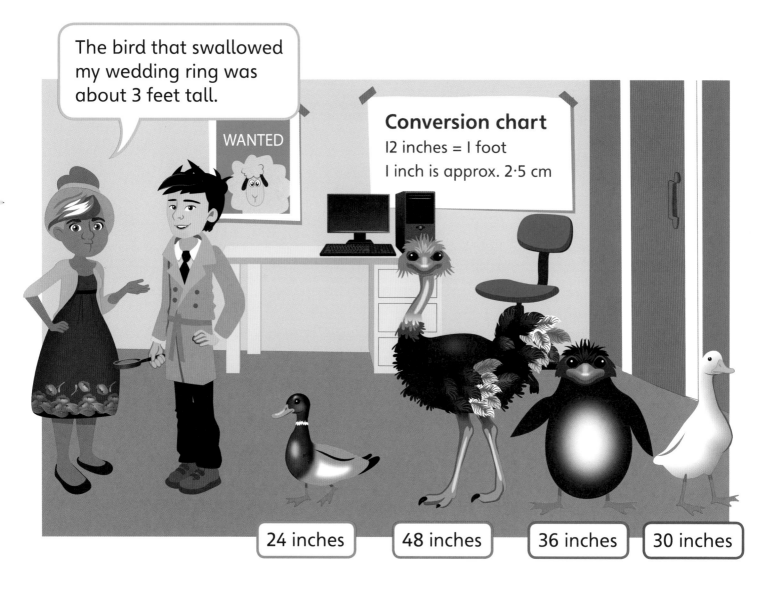

The bird that swallowed my wedding ring was about 3 feet tall.

WANTED

Conversion chart
12 inches = 1 foot
1 inch is approx. 2·5 cm

24 inches   48 inches   36 inches   30 inches

1 **a)** Which bird swallowed the ring?

b) How tall is the ostrich in metric units?

Share

a) **Inches** and **feet** are **imperial units** of length. 12 inches (in) = 1 foot (ft)

Imperial units were used in the UK until the metric system was introduced in 1965. The metric system made things easier as it deals with 10s, 100s and 1,000s. Imperial units are still sometimes used.

3 feet

1 foot	1 foot	1 foot
12 inches	12 inches	12 inches

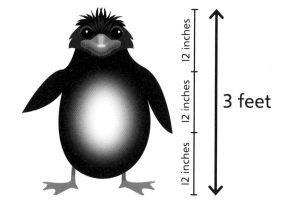

12 inches
12 inches
12 inches
3 feet

12 × 3 = 36

3 feet = 36 inches

The penguin swallowed the ring.

b) 1 inch is approximately 2·5 cm. The ostrich is 48 inches tall.

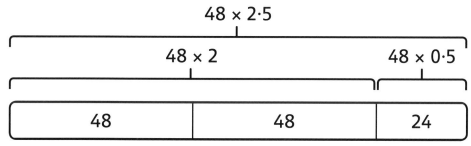

48 × 2·5

48 × 2   48 × 0·5

48	48	24

I know that 48 × 0·5 means 48 lots of $\frac{1}{2}$. This is the same as finding half of 48.

120 cm or 1·2 m

48 × 2 = 96

48 × 0·5 = 24

96 + 24 = 120 cm

120 ÷ 100 = 1·2 m

The ostrich is 120 cm tall, which is the same as 1·2 m.

Think together

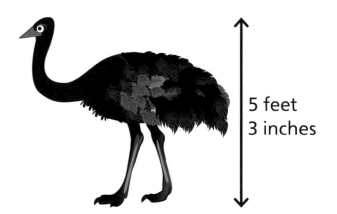

1 This emu is 5 feet and 3 inches tall. How tall is it in inches?

5 feet 3 inches

I foot (ft) = I2 inches (in)

5 feet 3 inches					
I foot	I foot	I foot	I foot	I foot	3 in
I2 inches	I2 inches	I2 inches	I2 inches	I2 inches	3 in

5 × I2   3

5 × I2 = ☐   ☐ + 3 = ☐

So, 5 feet 3 inches = ☐ inches. The emu is ☐ inches tall.

2 The duck's pond is I5 yards wide. How wide is it in inches?

I yard (yd) = 3 feet (ft)

I5 × ☐ = ☐

So, I5 yards = ☐ feet

☐ × ☐ = ☐

So, I5 yards = ☐ inches

The pond is ☐ inches wide.

I5 yds

I yd	I yd		
3 ft	3 ft		

I2 in · I2 in · I2 in · I2 in · I2 in · I2 in

I am going to multiply twice to find the answer: once to convert into feet and once to convert into inches.

3 Convert each of these imperial units into metric units.

Choose a range of metric units to convert to. For example, you could convert I inch into millimetres, I foot into centimetres and I yard into metres.

| I inch | I foot | I yard |

Explain how you can work out the answer.

Use these conversion facts to help.

I inch is about the same as 2·5 cm.

10 mm = I cm

12 inches = I foot

100 cm = I m

3 feet = I yard

1,000 m = I km

I wonder if I will need to convert all the measurements into inches first.

I am going to use the fact that I inch is about the same as $2\frac{1}{2}$ cm to help me.

167

Imperial units of mass

Discover

1 a) How many pounds of each type of fruit should Alex ask for?

b) What will the total of Alex's fruit weigh in kilograms?

Share

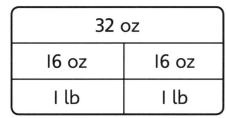

a)

> Pounds and ounces are imperial measures of mass. I pound (lb) equals 16 ounces (oz).

32 oz	
16 oz	16 oz
I lb	I lb

$32 \div 16 = 2$

$32\ oz = 2\ lb$

Alex should ask for 2 pounds of apples.

16 oz			
4 oz	4 oz	4 oz	4 oz

> I am going to see how many lots of 4 oz are in 16 oz to help with the second amount.

$1 \div 4 =$

I lb			
$\frac{1}{4}$ lb	$\frac{1}{4}$ lb	$\frac{1}{4}$ lb	$\frac{1}{4}$ lb

$4\ oz = \frac{1}{4}\ lb$

Alex should ask for $\frac{1}{4}$ of a pound of blueberries.

b) $32 + 4 = 36$

Alex's fruit will weigh 36 oz altogether.

> I know that I oz is about 28 g. First I am going to use long multiplication to convert into grams.

36×28

	20	8
30	600	240
6	120	48

$600 + 240 + 120 + 48 = 1{,}008$

Th	H	T	O
	6	0	0
	2	4	0
	1	2	0
+		4	8
1	0	0	8
		1	

$36 \times 28 = 1{,}008$ $1{,}008 \div 1{,}000 = 1{\cdot}008$

Alex's fruit will weigh about 1·008 kg.

169

Think together

15 ounces

1 How many grams of raspberries are there in one container?

1 oz	1 oz	1 oz	1 oz	1 oz	1 oz	1 oz	1 oz	1 oz	1 oz	1 oz	1 oz	1 oz	1 oz	1 oz
28 g	28 g	28 g												

15 oz

```
        2  8
   ×    1  5
   ─────────
   1  4 ₄0      28 × 5
   2  8  0      28 × 10
   ─────────
                28 × 15
```

$28 \times 15 = \boxed{}$

The raspberries weigh about $\boxed{}$ g.

2 **a)** There are 16 ounces in 1 pound.

1 lb															
1 oz	1 oz	1 oz	1 oz	1 oz	1 oz	1 oz	1 oz	1 oz	1 oz	1 oz	1 oz	1 oz	1 oz	1 oz	1 oz

Work out the number of ounces in these amounts.

4 lb $= \boxed{} \times \boxed{} = \boxed{}$ oz

10 lb $= \boxed{} \times \boxed{} = \boxed{}$ oz

$\frac{1}{2}$ lb $= \boxed{} \div \boxed{} = \boxed{}$ oz

b) Describe how you would find out what $\frac{3}{4}$ lb weighs in ounces.

3 **a)** Amelia is weighing a gift.

I lb is approximately 450 g.

I kg is approximately 2·2 lb.

What will the second set of scales show if Amelia weighs the gift using them?

I think I need to multiply 450 by 6 to find the answer.

I do not think that is right. I think you need to multiply 2·2 by 6 instead.

I **stone (st) = 14 lb**

b) How many pounds does the dog weigh?

Estimate the number of kilograms that the dog weighs.

171

Imperial units of capacity

Discover

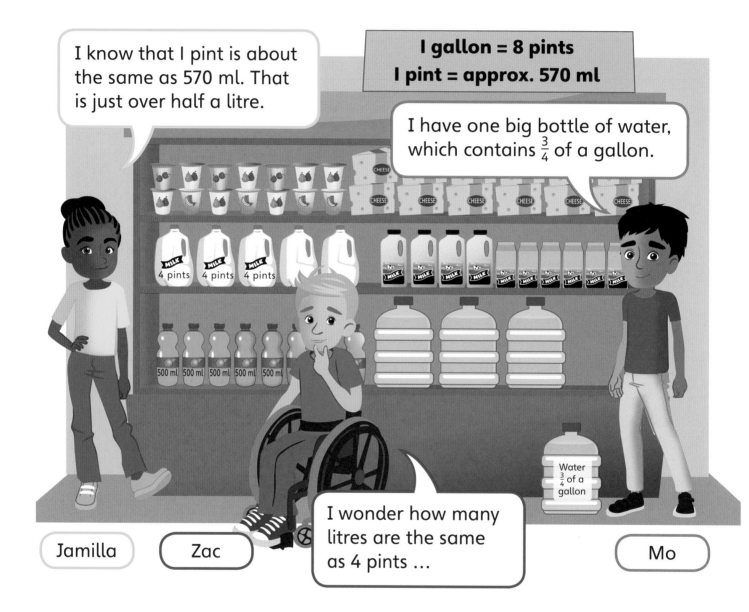

I know that I pint is about the same as 570 ml. That is just over half a litre.

I gallon = 8 pints
I pint = approx. 570 ml

I have one big bottle of water, which contains $\frac{3}{4}$ of a gallon.

4 pints 4 pints 4 pints

500 ml 500 ml 500 ml 500 ml 500 ml

Water $\frac{3}{4}$ of a gallon

I wonder how many litres are the same as 4 pints …

Jamilla   Zac   Mo

1 **a)** How many litres are approximately equal to 4 **pints** of milk?

   b) How many litres of water does Mo have?

Share

a) Pints and **gallons** are imperial units of capacity.

4 pints

I pint	I pint	I pint	I pint
570 ml	570 ml	570 ml	570 ml

$$
\begin{array}{r}
5\ 7\ 0 \\
\times \qquad 4 \\
\hline
2\ 2\ 8\ 0 \\
{\scriptstyle 2}
\end{array}
$$

> I am going to use short multiplication to find the total in millilitres. Then I will need to convert into litres.

Th	H	T	O	•	Tth	Hth	
2	2	8	0	•			ml
			2	•	2	8	l

$2{,}280 \div 1{,}000 = 2 \cdot 28$

2·28 litres are approximately equal to 4 pints of milk.

b) $\frac{3}{4}$ of a gallon = 6 pints

$$
\begin{array}{r}
5\ 7\ 0 \\
\times \qquad 6 \\
\hline
3\ 4\ 2\ 0 \\
{\scriptstyle 4}
\end{array}
$$

I gallon
8 pints

$8 \div 4 = 2$

2 pints	2 pints	2 pints	2 pints

$\frac{1}{4}$ of a gallon

$2 \times 3 = 6$

2 pints	2 pints	2 pints	2 pints

$\frac{3}{4}$ of a gallon

Mo has 3,420 millilitres of water.

$3{,}420 \div 1{,}000 = 3 \cdot 42$ Mo has 3·42 litres of water.

173

Think together

1 **a)** This water container holds 5 pints of water.

Approximately how many litres is this the same as?

5 pints

I pint	I pint	I pint	I pint	I pint
⬚ ml	⬚ ml	⬚ ml	⬚ ml	⬚ ml

$5 \times$ ⬚ $=$ ⬚

⬚ $\div 1{,}000 =$ ⬚

```
        ×        5
      _____

      _____
```

5 pints are about the same as ⬚ litres.

b) What is the difference between the capacity of the container and I gallon? Write your answer in litres.

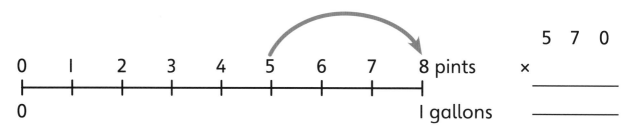

```
0   I   2   3   4   5   6   7   8 pints
├───┼───┼───┼───┼───┼───┼───┼───┤
0                               I gallons
```

```
        5   7   0
      ×
      _____

      _____
```

⬚ pints is the difference.

⬚ millilitres is the difference.

⬚ $\div 1{,}000 =$ ⬚

⬚ litres is the difference.

174

2 Is half a pint of milk more or less than a 330 ml can of lemonade?

I pint is approximately ⬜ ml.

⬜ ÷ 2 = ⬜

Half a pint is approximately ⬜ ml.

⬜ ml is _____ than 330 ml.

So half a pint of milk is _____ than a 330 ml can of lemonade.

3 Can you fill up the bucket using the water in the container?

Will there be any left?

 CHALLENGE

I gallon = 8 pints

I pint = approximately 570 ml

I gallon is 570 ml, so there is not enough water in the container to fill the bucket.

That is not right! You need to use the number of pints in a gallon to help.

175

Converting units of time

Discover

Toshi: I am taking my phone back to the shop. The charger has broken already and I have only had it 39 days!

Warning: Low Battery

On charge for 285 minutes

Amal: Buy one like mine! My battery has 5 bars and each bar takes an hour to charge.

Amal

1 a) How many weeks has Toshi had his phone for?

b) How many bars of Amal's battery should be charged fully?

How long until the next bar is charged?

Share

a)

There are 7 days in 1 week. 39 is not a multiple of 7, so I predict that there will be a remainder.

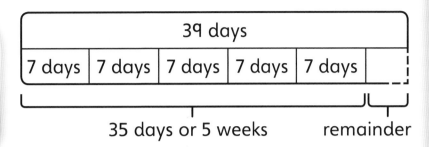

$39 \div 7 = 5$ remainder 4

So 39 days = 5 weeks and 4 days

Toshi has had his phone for 5 weeks and 4 days.

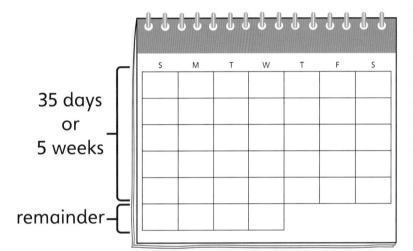

b) 60 minutes = 1 hour

285 minutes is between 240 and 300 minutes.

285 minutes = 4 hours and a remainder of minutes

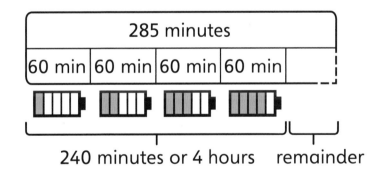

Amal's phone should have 4 bars fully charged.

$285 - 240 = 45$

Amal's phone has been charging for 4 hours and 45 minutes.

$60 - 45 = 15$

There are 15 minutes left until the next bar is charged.

Think together

1 Amal's phone is downloading updates. How many minutes has his phone been downloading updates for?

Downloading updates ...

378 seconds

```
0     1     2     3     4     5     6     7     minutes
├─────┼─────┼─────┼─────┼─────┼─────┼─────┤
0    60   120   [  ]  [  ]  [  ]  [  ]  [  ]   seconds
```

Count in 60s.

378 is between [ ] and [ ] .

So there are [ ] minutes and there will be a remainder of seconds.

378 − [ ] = [ ]

Amal's phone has been downloading for [ ] minutes and [ ] seconds.

2 How long until the sale ends?

Day 22 of our
5 week phone sale
Get in quick!
Ends soon

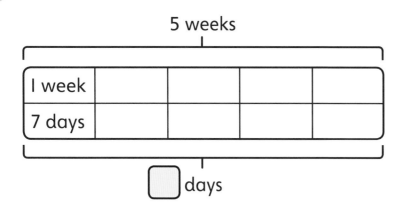

5 weeks

| 1 week | | | | |
| 7 days | | | | |

[ ] days

5 weeks = 5 × 7 = [ ] days

[ ] − 22 = [ ]

There are [ ] days left until the sale ends.

178

3 Jen's watch shows this time:

MON

13:00

In 24 hours, we will be on a ferry, sailing to Ireland!

In 30 hours, we will have arrived.

Jen

In 72 hours, we will be visiting my auntie.

Our ferry home is on Sunday at 11 pm.

In 93 hours, we will be going to a theme park.

a) What will Jen's watch look like at each of these times?

b) How many hours it is from the time on the watch until Jen returns on the ferry?

I know that there are 24 hours in a day. I can use the remainder to work out each time.

179

→ **Practice book 5C p132**

Timetables

Discover

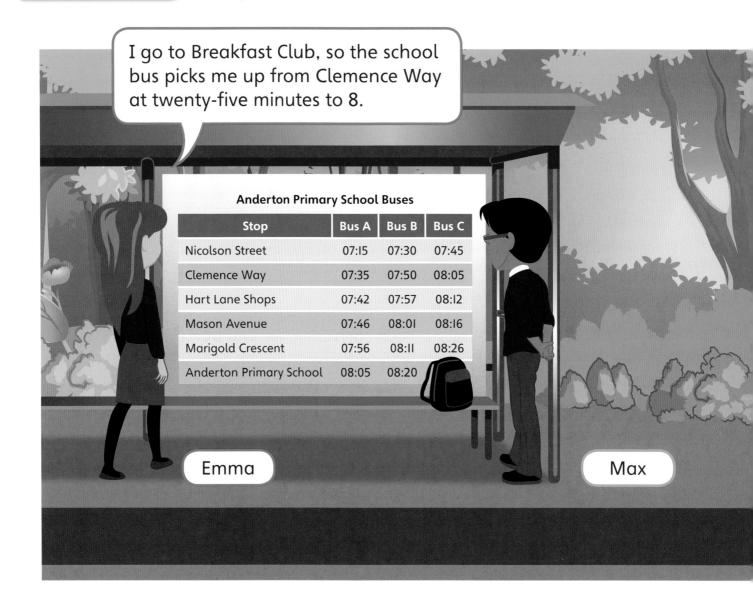

I go to Breakfast Club, so the school bus picks me up from Clemence Way at twenty-five minutes to 8.

Anderton Primary School Buses

Stop	Bus A	Bus B	Bus C
Nicolson Street	07:15	07:30	07:45
Clemence Way	07:35	07:50	08:05
Hart Lane Shops	07:42	07:57	08:12
Mason Avenue	07:46	08:01	08:16
Marigold Crescent	07:56	08:11	08:26
Anderton Primary School	08:05	08:20	

Emma

Max

① **a)** What time does Emma arrive at school?

b) All the buses take the same time to get to school. What time does Bus C arrive at school?

Share

a) Each column of the timetable shows a different bus. Each row shows a different place.

Timetables are usually written in 24-hour digital time, so you will have to convert first.

Stop	Bus A
Nicolson Street	07:15
Clemence Way	07:35
Hart Lane Shops	07:42
Mason Avenue	07:46
Marigold Crescent	07:56
Anderton Primary School	08:05

← Twenty-five minutes to 8
= 7:35 am
= 07:35

Emma catches Bus A. Emma arrives at school at 08:05 (five minutes past 8).

b)

I am going to use the information from the other buses to work out the hidden time.

Stop	Bus A	Bus B
Nicolson Street	07:15	07:30
Anderton Primary School	08:05	08:20

Bus A

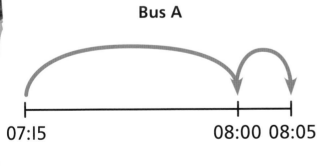

07:15   08:00 08:05

Bus C

07:45   08:00   08:35

+15 minutes   +35 minutes

+ 50 minutes

Each bus takes 50 minutes to get from Nicholson Street to school.

Bus C arrives at school at 08:35.

Think together

1 Look at this train timetable.

Littleborough	14:13	14:43	15:13	15:43
Birchfield	14:37	15:07	–	16:07
Ashtown Parkway	15:09	15:39	–	16:39
Ashtown Central	15:20	15:50	16:00	16:50

a) Lexi gets on the 15:07 train at Birchfield.

What time does she arrive in
Ashtown Central?

Lexi arrives in Ashtown Central

at [:] .

Littleborough	14:43
Birchfield	15:07
Ashtown Parkway	15:39
Ashtown Central	15:50

b) Andy gets on the 14:13 train at Littleborough.

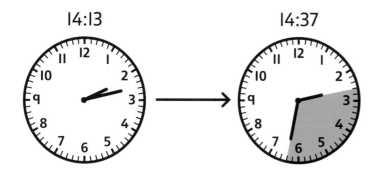

14:13   14:37

Littleborough	14:13
Birchfield	14:37
Ashtown Parkway	15:09
Ashtown Central	15:20

How long does it take to get to Birchfield?

It takes [ ] minutes to get to Birchfield.

2 How long does it take to get from Birchfield to Ashtown Parkway?

Littleborough	14:13
Birchfield	14:37
Ashtown Parkway	15:09
Ashtown Central	15:20

It takes ☐ minutes to get from Birchfield to Ashtown Parkway.

The journey crosses the o'clock boundary, so I am going to count in two jumps.

+ ☐ minutes

+ ☐ minutes   + ☐ minutes

14:37   15:00   15:09

3 The 15:13 train from Littleborough to Ashtown Central is an express train. It does not stop anywhere else.

CHALLENGE

Littleborough	15:13
Birchfield	–
Ashtown Parkway	–
Ashtown Central	16:00

I want to get from Littleborough to Ashtown Central as quickly as possible!

Aki

How much quicker is it for Aki to catch the express train than one of the other trains?

I am going to work out how long each journey is before finding the difference.

I think there is a quicker way. I can compare the departure and arrival times of the two journeys.

183

→ Practice book 5C p135

Problem solving – measure

Discover

I am going to make enough apple crumble for 5 people.

Lee

Oh dear! My scales only measure in grams!

Reena

I oz is approximately 28 grams

APPLE CRUMBLE
(Serves 4 people)

Ingredients
4 cooking apples
2 oz oats
4 oz brown sugar
5 oz plain flour
4 oz butter

1 a) How can Reena measure the ingredients using her scales?

b) What quantities should Lee use to make enough apple crumble for 5 people?

Share

a) Reena needs to convert from ounces (oz) to grams (g).

5 oz = 4 oz + 1 oz = 112 g + 28 g = 140 g

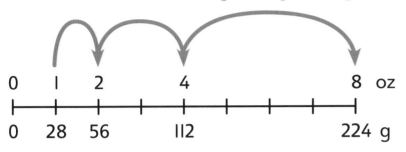

I could multiply each number by 28, but I can see a way to use doubling facts to help me multiply more quickly!

Reena can use the scales to measure these amounts:

2 oz = 56 g oats   4 oz = 112 g brown sugar
4 oz = 112 g butter   5 oz = 140 g plain flour

b) The recipe is for 4 people. Lee can divide each ingredient by 4 and multiply by 5.

I can divide by 4 to find the quantities for one person.
I will use this to alter the recipe for 5 people.

4 persons

1 person	1 person	1 person	1 person

1 person	1 person	1 person	1 person	1 person

5 persons

Ingredient	÷ 4 (one person)	× 5 (five people)
4 cooking apples	4 ÷ 4 = 1	1 × 5 = 5 cooking apples
56 g oats	56 ÷ 4 = 14 g	14 × 5 = 70 g oats
112 g brown sugar	112 ÷ 4 = 28 g	28 × 5 = 140 g brown sugar
112 g butter	112 ÷ 4 = 28 g	28 × 5 = 140 g butter
140 g plain flour	140 ÷ 4 = 35 g	35 × 5 = 175 g plain flour

Think together

1   Jamie wants to fill a 2 litre jug with milk.

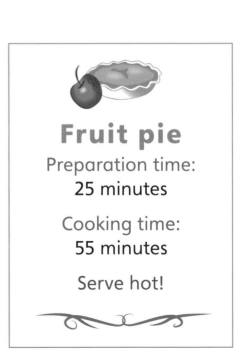

a) How many cartons of milk does she need to open to pour into the jug?

I pint is approximately 570 ml.

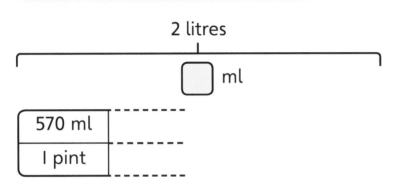

2 litres

[ ] ml

| 570 ml |
| I pint |

Jamie will need to open [ ] cartons of milk.

b) How much milk will Jamie have left over?

Jamie will have [ ] ml left over.

2   Danny is making a fruit pie.

He wants to serve it at 17:10.

Read the instructions. What is the latest time he should start preparing it?

Fruit pie
Preparation time:
25 minutes

Cooking time:
55 minutes

Serve hot!

3 These bags of sugar are all the same price.

A   B   C   D

Sugar 1·4 kg   Sugar 10 oz   Sugar 1,250 g   Sugar 2 lb

> 1 ounce (oz) is approximately 28 g.
>
> 1 pound (lb) is approximately 0·45 kg.

Which one is the best value?

Explain how to find the answer.

> It would be easier if all the bags were in the same unit of measurement.

> I know how to convert all these units into grams. I could then compare them.

187

End of unit check

1 There are 9·2 litres of water in a fish tank. How many millilitres is this?

A 9·2000 ml   B 920 ml   C 9,200 ml   D 0·0092 ml

2 Which of these statements is not correct?

A To convert from grams into kilograms, divide by 1,000.

B To convert from kilograms into grams, multiply by 1,000.

C To convert from kilograms into grams, divide by 1,000.

D There are 2,000 grams in 2 kilograms.

3 A marathon runner takes 3 hours and 48 minutes to complete the race.

How many minutes is this?

A 3·48 minutes   C 348 minutes

B 180 minutes   D 228 minutes

4 Bella has three bags of rice weighing 1·2 kg, 200 g and 5 kg. What mass of rice does she have in total?

A 6·4 kg   B 1,405 g   C 206·2 kg   D 820 g

5 This is part of a bus timetable.

Bus Station	08:47	08:57	09:07	09:17	09:27
Kingsway	08:52	09:02	09:12	09:22	09:32
Mount Pleasant	09:04	09:14	09:24	09:34	09:44
High Street	09:11	09:21	09:31	09:41	09:51
Oakfield Avenue	09:15	09:25	09:35	09:45	09:55
Leisure Centre	09:25	09:35	09:45	09:55	10:05

Ambika wants to catch a bus from Kingsway to the Leisure Centre. She needs to be at the Leisure Centre at five minutes to 10.

What time should she catch the bus?

A 9:17 am   **B** 9:22 am   **C** 9:32 am   **D** 9:22 pm

6 This piece of string is being measured in inches. What is its length in centimetres?

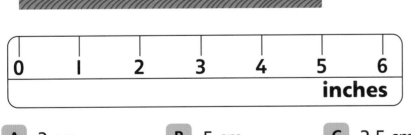

A 2 cm   **B** 5 cm   **C** 2·5 cm   **D** 12·5 cm

7 These durations show the length of time a bus takes between stops.

300 seconds $\frac{1}{4}$ of an hour $4\frac{1}{2}$ minutes   5 minutes 10 seconds

Put the lengths of time in order, from shortest to longest.

189

→ **Practice book 5C p141**

Unit 17
Measure – volume and capacity

In this unit we will …
- ⚡ Learn what the volume of a shape is
- ⚡ Find volumes of shapes by counting unit cubes
- ⚡ Draw shapes with different volumes
- ⚡ Compare the volume of different shapes
- ⚡ Estimate the capacity of different shapes

How many unit cubes are used to make this cube?

We will need some maths words. Which of these are new?

volume   cube   cuboid   3D shape

solid   capacity   calculate

estimate   unit cubes

least   greatest

Which container do you think has the greatest capacity? Why?

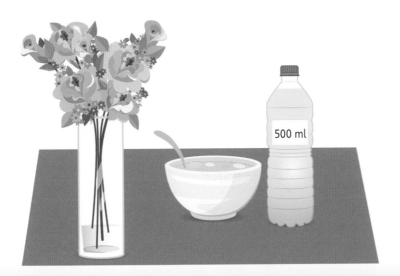

500 ml

What is volume?

Discover

I think our cubes have the same volume.

Our shapes look different, though.

Reena

Zac

1 **a)** Is Zac correct?

What do you think is meant by **volume**?

b) Build three other 3D shapes using cubes that have the same volume as Zac and Reena's shapes.

Share

a)

Volume means the amount of space that an object fills. We can use **unit cubes** as a way to measure volume.

I am going to count the number of unit cubes in each shape.

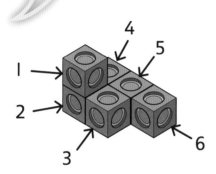

Reena's cube uses 6 cm cubes.

It has a volume of 6 unit cubes.

I think one of the cubes in Zac's shape is hidden.

Zac's shape also uses 6 unit cubes.

It has the same volume as Reena's shape.

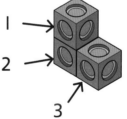
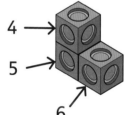

b) Each of these shapes has a volume of 6 unit cubes, the same volume as Reena's and Zac's shapes.

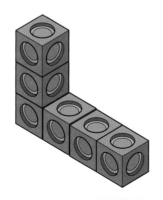

Think together

1 What is the volume of each shape?

a)

Volume = ☐ unit cubes

b)

Volume = ☐ unit cubes

c)

Volume = ☐ unit cubes

d)

Volume = ☐ unit cubes

2 Using 12 cubes, build three different 3D shapes.

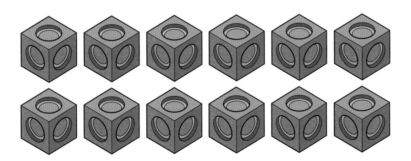

I am going to try to make a cuboid.

③

Drawing 3D shapes is challenging.

Reena

We can use isometric paper. It makes it a bit easier.

Zac

a) On isometric paper, draw more cubes like this one.

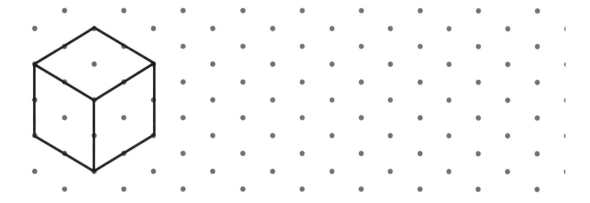

b) Draw the following 3D shapes on isometric paper.

What is the volume of each of your shapes?

These look difficult to draw. I may need to make a few attempts. I know I will be able to do it though.

That is a great attitude to have.

→ Practice book 5C p143

Comparing volumes

Discover

My shape is the tallest, so it must have the greatest volume.

Andy   Emma   Isla

1 a) Who has built the 3D shape with the greatest volume?

b) Isla adds more cubes to her shape so that it has the same volume as Emma's shape.

What could Isla's shape look like now?

Share

a) Andy and Emma have made cuboids. Isla's shape is irregular.

Andy's shape

Isla's shape

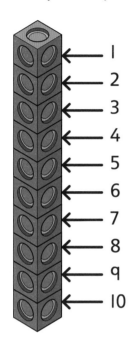

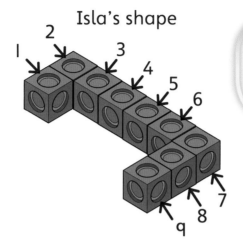

I counted the cubes in each shape.

Emma's shape

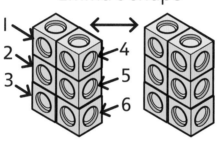

I split Emma's shape into 2 layers. There are 6 cubes in each layer.

$6 \times 2 = 12$ unit cubes.

Andy's shape has a volume of 10 unit cubes.
Isla's shape has a volume of 9 unit cubes.
Emma's shape has a volume of 12 unit cubes.

$9 < 10 < 12$

Emma has built the shape with the greatest volume.

b) Isla's shape has 9 cubes. Emma's shape has 12. Isla needs to add 3 more cubes for her shape to have the same volume as Emma's. It might look like one of these two shapes.

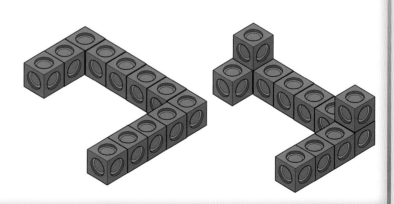

Think together

1 Isla and Emma make another two shapes.
Whose shape has the smaller volume?

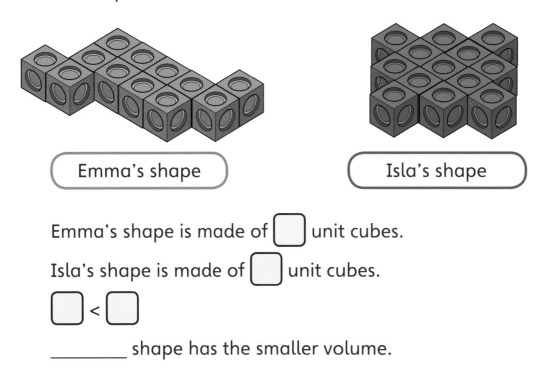

Emma's shape

Isla's shape

Emma's shape is made of ⬜ unit cubes.

Isla's shape is made of ⬜ unit cubes.

⬜ < ⬜

_____ shape has the smaller volume.

2 Order these shapes from least to greatest volume.

A   B   C

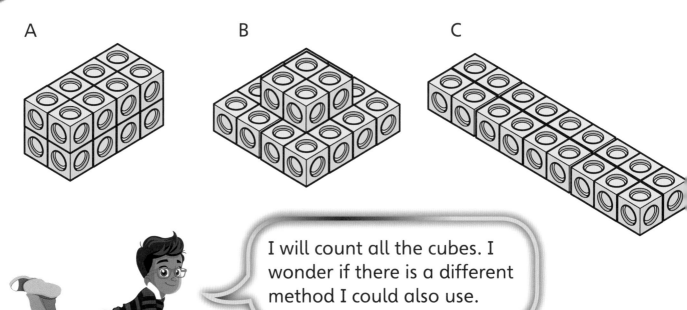

I will count all the cubes. I
wonder if there is a different
method I could also use.

3 **a)** Andy and Emma have made some more 3D shapes.

I think my shape has a larger volume as I have used more cubes.

Are you sure? I think our shapes have the same volume.

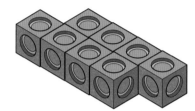

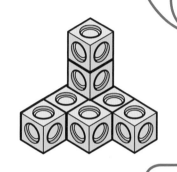

Andy

Emma

Who is correct? Explain your answer.

b) Isla makes the following shape, using bigger cubes.

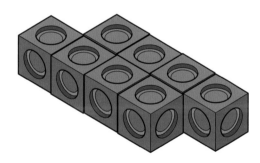

Does Isla's shape have the same volume as Andy's?

They must have the same volume as they have the same number of cubes.

They have the same number of cubes, but Isla's cubes do not look the same size as Andy's.

→ Practice book 5C p146

Estimating volume

Discover

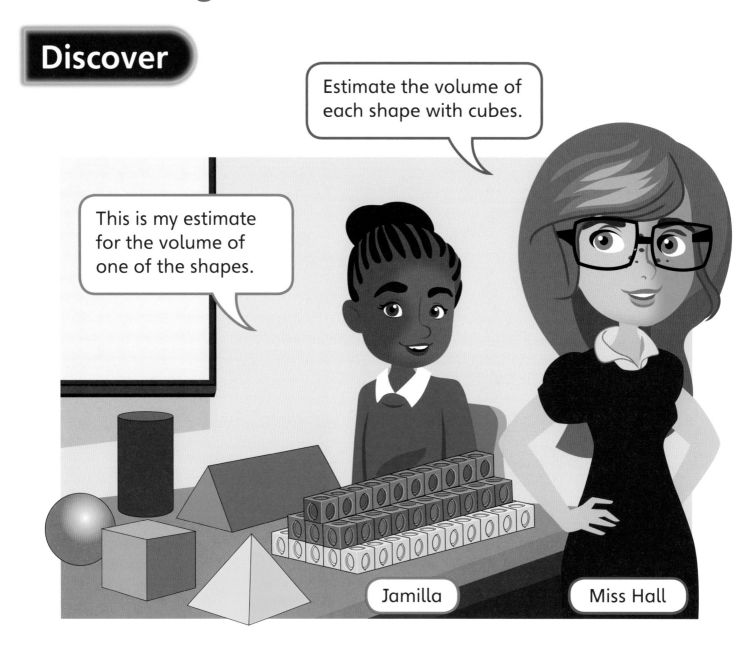

Estimate the volume of each shape with cubes.

This is my estimate for the volume of one of the shapes.

Jamilla

Miss Hall

1 **a)** Which 3D shape did Jamilla estimate the volume of?

What is the estimate of the volume of the shape?

b) Why is it only an estimate?

Share

a) Jamilla estimated the volume of the triangular prism by making a shape out of cubes that could fit inside it.

> I worked out the volume of each layer and added them together.

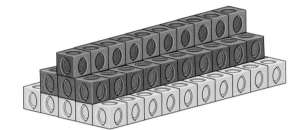

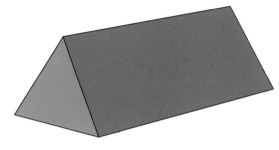

$10 \times 1 = 10$ cubes

$10 \times 3 = 30$ cubes

$10 \times 5 = 50$ cubes

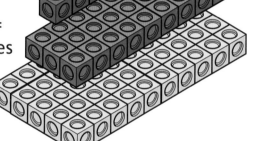

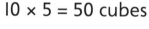

$50 + 30 + 10 = 90$ unit cubes

> I tried another way. I worked out the volume in each 'slice' and multiplied.

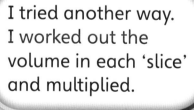

$10 \times 9 = 90$ unit cubes

An estimate of the volume of the triangular prism is 90 unit cubes.

b) The volume is an estimate because it is not exact, as there would still be spaces left in the triangular prism if it were filled with the cubes.

> The volume of the 3D shape is likely to be a bit more than 90 cubes.

Think together

1   Use the models to estimate the volume of each of the 3D shapes.

a)

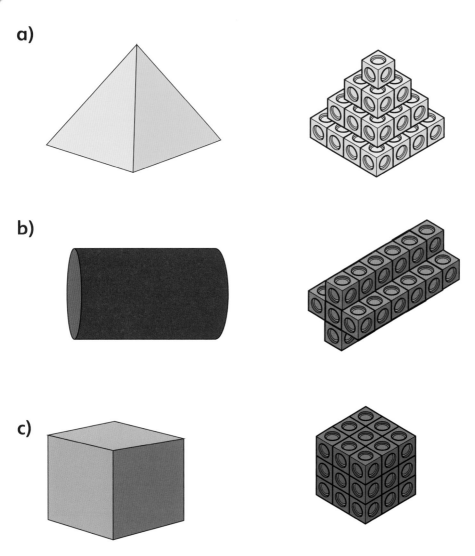

b)

c)

Which do you think is the most accurate estimate of the volume? Explain your answer.

2   Pick an object in your classroom.

How can you use cubes to estimate the volume of the object?

3 **a)** Discuss how to compare the volume of each ball.

I will make a model of each shape with cubes.

b)

The football is about three times as tall as the tennis ball, so I think the volume will be three times greater, too.

Reena

Do you agree with Reena?

I will imagine each ball is a cube.

203

Estimating capacity

Discover

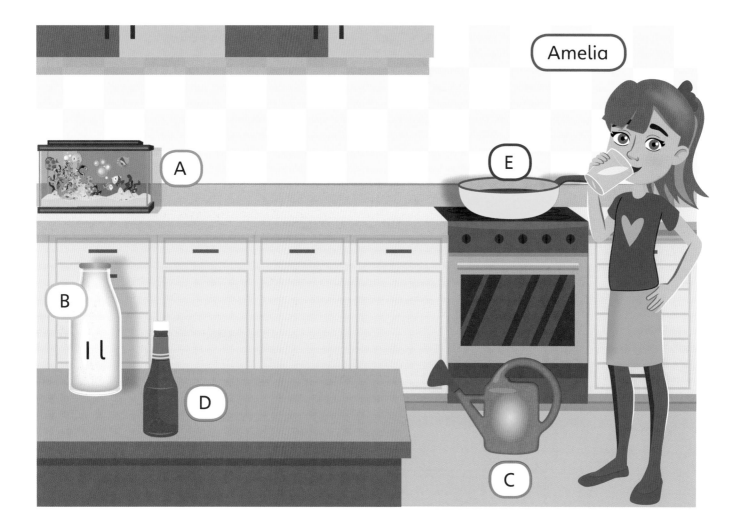

1 **a)** How much water do you estimate Amelia's glass will hold?

b) There are five containers in the kitchen, labelled A to E.

Put these containers in order, from the one with the smallest capacity to the one with the greatest capacity.

Share

a)

I know that a can of soft drink holds between 250 ml and 330 ml.

The glass looks like it holds slightly less. I estimate it holds 200 ml of water.

330 ml

You can estimate that the glass holds between 180 ml and 250 ml of water.

b)

There is a label on the milk. It says 1 l. This means 1 litre.

The ketchup bottle looks like it holds less than the milk bottle. It is not as wide or as tall.

The pan, watering can and fish tank hold more water than the milk bottle.

Smallest capacity ←————————————→ Greatest capacity

Think together

Capacity is how much a container can hold.

1 Choose the best estimate of the capacity of each of these items.

a)

b)

| 500 ml | 2 ml | 5 l | 2 l | 500 l | 20 l |

2 100 ml of juice has been poured into each glass.

Estimate the capacity of each glass.

A

B

C

D

3 **a)** How can Danny measure the capacity of the colander?

Danny

I think there might be a way to use cubes to estimate.

I wonder if you could use rice or sand.

b) Discuss different methods for estimating the capacity of these containers accurately.

207

→ Practice book 5C p152

End of unit check

 1 What is the volume of this shape?

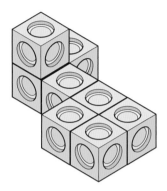

- **A** 8 unit cubes
- **B** 7 unit cubes
- **C** 9 unit cubes
- **D** 17 units cubes

 2 Which shape does not have the same volume as the other shapes?

A

C

B

D

 3 Which shape has the greatest volume?

A

C

B

D

4 What is the most suitable estimate for a can of soft drink?

A 30 ml B 330 ml C 3 l D 30 l

5 300 ml of juice has been poured into the glass.
Estimate the capacity of the glass.

A 300 ml C 700 ml

B 400 ml D I l

6 This jug was full. Now a pint has been poured from it. Use this
information to estimate the number of ml in one pint.

— 2 l

7 Estimate how many spheres of this size will fit in the box.
Explain your workings.

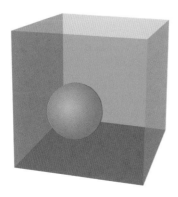

→ **Practice book 5C p155**

I have enjoyed the challenge of this book!

Holiday fun

Here are some ideas you can try at home.

Architecture

You will need: newspaper, sticky tape, imagination and engineering skills.

Roll up sheets of newspaper to make strong tubes. From these tubes, construct a building. Your design could look like a famous building such as the Eiffel Tower or the Eden Project.

Alternatively, you could design a futuristic skyscraper, or your dream house. How about a bridge that can cross more than 2 metres?

How long is left?

Work out how long is left until the end of your summer holiday.

How many weeks? What about how many days … minutes … hours … seconds?

How many hours will you spend asleep? Or eating?

If you are travelling somewhere by car, bus, boat or plane, estimate the number of minutes the journey will take. Compare your estimates with other people in your family.

Measuring

Plan a hiking expedition with an adult from your family. Use suitable maps and read the scales carefully to accurately judge the distances and plan your rest-stops. Work out how many miles, metres or km your walk will be, and how many litres of water you will need to take with you. How much will your backpack weigh, once it is full of supplies?

Estimate how long the walk will take, and judge the best time to set off and your expected return time.

Mathematical art

Try this challenge. Draw a pattern of shapes. The shapes can overlap or can be split with straight lines. The lines can be curved or straight or a mixture. The important thing is that there are some gaps to colour in. Now take some colouring pens or pencils and colour the pattern so that no two adjacent areas are the same colour. What is the fewest number of colours you can use?

Now try creating a design where you draw a long line that can twist and turn and overlap, but where you do not take your pen or pencil from the page until the design is finished. How many different colours do you need for this design?

I enjoy listening to my partners to learn from them.

It is great to share ideas!

What have we learnt?

Can you do all these things?

⚡ Add and subtract decimals

⚡ Identify decimal sequences

⚡ Problem-solve using decimals

⚡ Multiply and divide decimals by 10, 100 and 1,000

⚡ Measure with a protractor

⚡ Calculate angles

⚡ Recognise properties and positions of shapes

⚡ Understand positions and directions of shapes

⚡ Measure and convert units

⚡ Understand measures of volume and capacity

Some of it was difficult, but we did not give up!

Now you are ready for the next books!

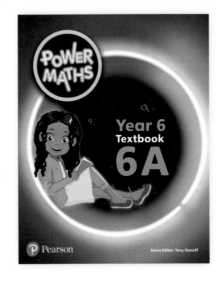

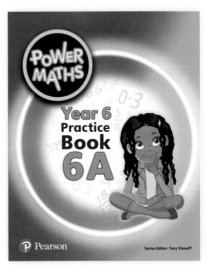